Can't Buy Me Love

Freedom from Compulsive Spending and Money Obsession

Can't Buy Me Love

By Sally Coleman, M.S., M.A.,
and Nancy Hull-Mast

FAIRVIEW PRESS
Minneapolis

Published by Fairview Press 2450 Riverside Avenue South Minneapolis, MN 55454.

Library of Congress Cataloging-in-Publication Data

Coleman, Sally.
    Can't buy me love: freedom from compulsive spending and money obsession/Sally Coleman and Nancy Hull-Mast
        p. cm.
    Includes bibliographical references.
    ISBN 0-925190-46-2
    1. Compulsive shopping. 2. Hoarding of money—Psychological aspects. I. Hull-Mast, Nancy. II. Title.
RC569.5.S56C65 1993   92-37139
616.85'227—dc20   CIP

Cover design: Circus Design

99 98 97 96 95   6 5 4 3 2 1

Publisher's Note: Fairview Press publishes books and other materials related to the subjects of physical health, mental health, and chemical dependency. Its publications, including Can't Buy Me Love, do not necessarily reflect the philosophy of Fairview Hospital and Healthcare Services or their treatment programs.
For a current catalog of Fairview Press titles, please call toll-free, 1-800-544-8207.

The stories and themes contained in this book have been derived from our own private experiences, informal research, and clinical observation. In our respect for confidentiality, vignettes concerning people in this text are composites taken from the stories of money addicts. They do not refer to specific individuals. All names and identifying characteristics have been fictionalized and completely altered.

Out of suffering have emerged the strongest souls; the most massive characters are seared with scars.

E. H. Chapin

Contents

PART THREE

Foreword

As a psychiatrist and medical director of a large midwestern hospital, I first encountered an identified "money addict" about four years ago. A local therapist had referred a man to me who was significantly depressed because of his out of control shopping and spending. At first I thought the therapist was inventing a new concept. As I looked deeper I found that the patient's problem had progressed until currently he was opening up an average of one checking account per day to cover other banks' checks that were ready to bounce. As a result, he faced a jail sentence for forging checks and repeatedly overdrawing his bank accounts. His marriage was also on the brink of dissolution.

I was fascinated by the parallels to alcoholism in the patient's behavior. He told a detailed story about covering his checks, making plans for his next shopping spree, and developing complicated schemes to find money for continued spending. I still suspected that his spending abuse was secondary to an underlying depression or craving for affection and that an appropriate mix of therapy and medications would enable the patient to stop spending and recover. However, as I spent more time with him in the hospital trying to understand his behavior, it became obvious that he displayed a primary pattern of addictive behavior parallel to what I'd seen in patients with other addictions. His depression also followed a pattern similar to that in some patients who are depressed secondarily to their addiction; once they gain better control over their addiction, their depression improves. (Other patients have a dual diagnosis, with the presence of depression as a disorder separate from the addiction.) This patient's depression significantly improved when he began to spend part of his day on the chemical dependency unit addressing his money addiction.

Over the subsequent years, I have been able to identify patients with shopping and spending addictions rather readily. The addiction model has proven to be extremely helpful. The following two cases illustrate this problem and its subtlety.

A thirty-nine-year-old married man, father of two children, was referred to me by his physician for hyper sexual behavior, pressured speech, and irritability of mood. His referring physician, suspecting hypo mania, wanted a second opinion, as well as treatment if the diagnosis was confirmed. In my first encounter with that patient, he admitted to the above symptoms, denied any symptoms of depression, and minimized the need for treatment, stating that his family problems bothered him more than any of his other symptoms. The patient refused to return for follow-up.

Six months later the patient was brought to the hospital after a suicide attempt by carbon monoxide poisoning. During that hospitalization he described a pattern of sexual addiction. He reported that he had survived an attempted molestation in his early teens. Upon questioning, he also confirmed a history of occasional alcohol abuse, which resulted in occasional blackouts and difficulty in his marriage.

When this pattern of addictions secondary to an abusive childhood emerged, I asked the patient about any other addictions that he might have. He unraveled a very extensive debt history with spending sprees that typically were associated with days when he felt depressed and unloved. This behavior had resulted in a $13,000 debt that his wife was unaware of, owed through several credit cards and a bank account.

When this information came to light, the necessity for drastic change became obvious. Only a plan to pay down the debt would enable the patient and his wife to work out their financial problems. Financial arrangements were made that restricted the patient's ability to borrow and to play games with money. These practical agreements were part of his treatment plan. He accepted his addiction patterns and finally began to attend support groups for sexual addiction and spending addiction. He continued individual therapy as well, to work through the sexual abuse by a neighbor that he now recognized. His moods are now much more clearly related to his memories and feelings about that abuse and are managed without the use of medication.

The second case involves a professional woman in her late fifties married to a prominent person. The couple came in for treatment following the psychiatric hospitalization of their thirty-three-year-old daughter. She was identified as suffering from both mixed bipolar disorder and dependence on alcohol and prescription drugs. The family was in denial regarding the extent of her drug abuse. During family therapy sessions, when we asked about any other history of addiction in the family, the parents cited only a maternal aunt's problem with alcohol. Not being satisfied with that answer, we ran down a list of possible other addictions. At this point, the mother broke down and admitted her compulsive shopping and spending. Understanding these addictive behaviors helped greatly in family therapy.

After I read a draft of this book, I learned about poverty addiction and realized that this concept explains the behavior exhibited by the father of one of my patients, a teenage girl. The fresh insight illustrates the usefulness of this book to mental health professionals. My patient's father is fifty years old. He has a nicotine addiction, having tried and failed repeatedly to control his smoking habit. He also has had periods when he abused alcohol and was advised by his physician to stop using it because of its effect on his liver, although he reported that he hasn't gotten drunk, missed work, or had any legal consequences as a result of his drinking. This man describes a very abusive man, the patient's grandfather, who raised him with the sense that he was worthless and that only his younger brother had any meaning in the grandfather's life. This brother died at a young age of cancer, which left the survivors trapped together in anger, frustration, and emotional deprivation.

In addition to his abuse of chemicals, my patient's father admits an addiction to buying things on sale and hoarding them for later use. In the past, he constantly had the urge to go to garage sales and close-out stores to get the best bargains and buy the cheapest items he could find. He spent all of his time shopping, neglecting his family even when they were ill. Currently he persists in depriving himself and his family. He drives cars that he buys at auctions from bank foreclosures, and he continues to fix them until they are ready to be towed to the junkyard, even though he could afford to buy a new car every year. He has a large retirement fund and a large inheritance, and his income is in the top ten percent of the population. Understanding his poverty addiction and obsession with deprivation is providing essential missing links in the treatment of his daughter and the family as a whole.

I chose the above cases to illustrate the interplay between various addictions in the same family or the same individuals and the relationship between mood disorders and multiple addictions. Based on my experience to date, I have decided to ask referred patients detailed questions about their addictions to substances or activities, including alcohol, street drugs, prescription drugs, money, gambling, eating, working, and sexual addiction. Frequently it helps to ask a person close to the patient about those addictions because the patient may deny problems. A spouse or children might reveal a more complete picture.

I suspect that the etiology of this addiction is very similar to that of alcohol and drug addiction. There are multifactorial conditions associated with genetic disposition and learned behavior; quite often addicts have a history of an abusive or dysfunctional childhood. Perhaps the choice of money obsession has to do with the social acceptability of spending as a "soothing' behavior. The proliferation of shopping malls and readily available credit cards during the last few decades has doubtless stimulated compulsive spending.

Understanding the dynamics of money obsession and spending abuse and addiction has proven immensely helpful in my medical practice. It is my hope that this phenomenon will be taken into account by more professionals in the mental health and addictions field.

Suhayl Nasr, M.D.
Medical Director,Kingwood Hospital
Michigan City, Indiana

Acknowledgments

For . . .

Sally Coleman; it has been an honor to work with you.
My mother, Barbara Kingwill, the most courageous woman I know.
My husband, Steven Mast, the richest man in town.

Nancy Hull-Mast

The finest gift my mother gave me was the gift of encouragement. From the time I could hold a pencil she praised me for every piece of writing and drawing I brought to her. She didn't have the opportunity to fulfill her personal dreams. I thank and bless her for believing in mine. I also thank and bless Jack, who encouraged me to begin writing again.

I would also like to thank my coauthor, Nancy Hull-Mast, who is able to listen with her heart. Nancy's active commitment to making the world a good and just place for her children and others has been an inspiration to observe. Many people talk about what they believe in— Nancy has the courage to act as well as speak out for what she believes.

Sally Coleman

We wish to thank our editor, Jane Resh Thomas, for her positive, wise, and creative suggestions and her overall commitment to excellence. We also thank Professor Teresa Ghilarducci of the University of Notre Dame Economics Department. Her insights, openness, and zest for this subject energized us. We are also grateful to Dr. Suhayl Nasr for his medical insight and compassion as a human being open to new learning. We thank the staff at Deerpath Secretarial Services for their fine work and their patience. Finally, we express our gratitude to our agent, Jane Jordan Browne, for her persistence and belief in the value of our book.

Introduction

Nancy Hull-Mast and her husband, Steve, were just about to bolt, having given final instructions to the baby sitter, when the phone rang and she answered it. When Steve saw her purse fall from her shoulder and her posture change from anticipated flight to settling in, he knew something important was brewing on the other end of the line.

Nancy hadn't heard from Clair in over a year, but within minutes they had reconnected as soul mates. Clair said she was in deep trouble, living a life of extreme fear. She no longer slept peacefully at night because she was convinced that her creditors would find her and somehow take her away in shame. The resulting scandal would destroy her family. As she spoke, Nancy began to recognize her story as familiar yet altogether new. What Clair described was a progression of events like those Nancy had been writing about for more than ten years. The themes characterized addiction, but the details were unlike anything she had previously researched.

Although she knew about the loss of control associated with the use of alcohol and other drugs, Nancy had never connected the phenomenon with the use of money. By her own admission, Clair was out of control. Nancy also was familiar with the addict's inability to predict accurately the amount of alcohol, drugs, or food he would use on any given occasion. Now Clair was talking about a similar powerlessness, but this time the problem was a substance called money. If Nancy had known then what she knows now, she could have referred Clair to Debtors Anonymous (DA), but all she could do that muggy July evening was listen for a few minutes.

Her friend was suffering and didn't know where to turn. Some would say, well, too bad, it was her own fault, but there was much more to the story. Clair was not a selfish person. She was an intelligent woman with a good heart. Her trouble went a lot deeper than the societal dismissal of some "silly female" who shopped too much.

Nancy's curiosity piqued, she asked Sally Coleman whether she thought that money misuse could itself be a process similar to addiction as well as an expression of psychological pain. Sally is a psychotherapist with over twenty years of clinical experience and the coordinator of addiction services at the University of Notre Dame Counseling Center. Not only did she concur with Nancy's hypothesis, she already had begun putting her ideas on the subject to paper and as early as 1982 had written one of the first articles published on this subject for *Alcoholism Magazine*.[1] She called money the "last taboo," saying that clients would rather discuss and change just about anything other than their obsessive relationship with money. When many of them did open up, she heard language that addicts use to describe their compulsions:

- "Why can't I stop spending?"
- "I worry about and horde money continually, even though I'm not in any financial trouble."
- "I don't want to look at my spending—it's the only thing I have left to enjoy."
- "I lie awake each night worrying about my creditors."
- "I feel guilty when I spend even a little money."
- "What's wrong with me? I take cash advances against one credit card to pay another."
- "Denial about my money problems ruined my marriage."

Sally has seen money problems undermine the lives of her clients from varied socioeconomic and cultural backgrounds. She observes that the real issue is not how much or how little money a person has but rather the manner in which the individual uses money, the resultant life disruptions, and the underlying motivations for spending patterns.

Whether people are buying yachts or yarn, the resulting emotional fallout can be the same. Sally has observed several broad categories of money addiction, primarily including overspending and underspending, and Nancy's own interviews with members of DA also bear out her perceptions. *Poverty addict* is the term DA uses to describe one who underspends and purposely does without to the extreme. When Nancy first heard this term from a woman she was interviewing, her reaction was, "Who the heck would get a *good feeling* from poverty?" Her interviewee was a patient person who overlooked the interviewer's ignorance and answered her question. She told Nancy that many DA members consider themselves to be poverty addicts.

Although poverty addicts are as dysfunctional about money as compulsive spenders are, we have focused more on the latter group in this book. Our emphasis is not an oversight. The behavior of the deprivation obsessed poverty addict is life-involving, but when an overspender is in the throes of the spending process, it involves not only family and close friends but a cast of many others. Often angry creditors, lenders, and landlords come into the matter. Sales clerks, bank representatives, and collection agencies enter the situation, too. Even the police, lawyers, and other officials may become involved. Bankruptcies increased twenty-five percent between 1990 and 1991 as our nation spiraled into deeper cycles of debt and overspending.[2] In other words, there are more overspenders than underspenders. Those in the former group also make more noise and more often are involved in situations that are incompatible with the poverty addict's lower-profile lifestyle of deprivation and scarcity.

The flip side of the poverty addiction coin could be described as "wealth addiction." In her best-selling book, *When Society Becomes an Addict*, Anne Wilson Schaef writes about this issue:

"In our culture the process of accumulating money often becomes addictive. Like any other addiction it is progressive; it takes more and more to achieve a fix, and eventually no amount is enough People . . . often do not care about money in and of itself; what drives them is the series of actions and interactions involved in accumulating it."[3]

Wealth addiction is the enactment of an obsessive and compulsive need to acquire money and wealth, or at least the focusing on these matters. Money ideally brings personal freedom and satisfaction. Problems occur when a person's excesses cause a pattern of disruptions in primary areas of their lives.

One woman interviewed for this book, a recovering alcoholic, spoke of her husband Paul and the pain-filled years of their marriage: "Money became Paul's god. For years he gave all of himself to making more and more money. We had all the material possessions but little family connection and real sharing. The enemy in our marriage was not another woman; it was Paul's consuming affair with money. When I complained he always replied, Well, it's all for you and the kids.' "

And what of this word *addict*? Are people addicted to their use of money and compelled to this style of life, or are they freely choosing it? The authors looked at this question very carefully before deciding whether the terms *addict* and *addiction* have a place in this book. In tracing the progression of money problems with her clients, Sally has found the addictions model of diagnosis to be invaluable. It conceptualizes the chaos and gives a workable and defining framework to the daily experiences of someone caught in the cycle of overspending, restrictive spending, and other money obsessions.

Viewing these obsessions and compulsions as an addiction does not *excuse* behavior but instead gives the suffering person a model whereby to understand and change out-of-control behavior. When the addictive acting out stops, client and therapist can see clearly the underlying causation. As it is essential for the alcoholic first to stop drinking, the money addict likewise must stop abusing money in order to begin to grow emotionally and spiritually. The addiction framework is a practical footing for such a beginning. Defining behavior that is out of control as an addiction provides a foundation for healing and accountability.

The compulsive use of money shares many features with alcohol use that is out of control. The authors see alcoholism as an addiction to both substance and process; the alcoholic gets physically and emotionally high with the use of the substance, alcohol. Money addicts don't necessarily get physically high, but their involvement in the dramatic compulsive cycle of money obsession does result in an emotional high. Money addiction could therefore be described as *a progressive, life-disrupting process of obsession with money and its uses, which results in a pattern of highs and lows; eventually the addict loses control of the ability to use money as planned.*

In his classic exploration of the psychology of addiction, Gerald May, M.D., extends this definition:

All of our addictions, even our non-substance addictions, share similar dynamics. And the most serious of our non-substance addictions even share a similarly ominous potential addiction to power, money, or relationships which can drive people to distort reality just as much as can an addiction to alcohol or narcotics.[4]

The pioneering work of Patrick Carnes, Ph. D., which describes and defines sexual addiction, supports this concept that addictions to processes share similar dynamics with substance abuse:

Addictive compulsivity had many forms other than alcohol and drug abuse. Also, the different forms— overeating, gambling, sexuality, buying, shoplifting— all shared a similar process. And in addition, within the family addictions would be like overlays whose reinforcing shadows simply deepened the patterns of family pathology.[5]

As the authors sought the courage to speak of money obsession in terms of addiction, they were aware of criticisms that would be raised against this concept. "What? Another addiction? People can justify anything by calling it an addiction!" The addiction model has proven one of the most helpful treatment and self-help frameworks of this century. Only after much deliberation and counsel have the authors used this model to conceptualize obsessive, uncontrolled use of money. This position is not an "excuse" for unhealthy behaviors or a blanket to hide other important underlying psycho dynamics. The addiction framework fits best and is the most helpful to clients, clinicians, and others as a practical program of recovery. Over the years, Sally's clients have benefited from understanding how their money patterns resembled an addictive illness. This approach is consistent with the Twelve Steps of DA and with the few hospital based and outpatient treatment programs specifically sensitive to money abuse and addiction at this time.

Little research has been conducted into the emotional disruptions caused by money obsessions and compulsions, even though clinicians have been observing and writing about this dynamic for years. Disagreements about sex, children, and money consistently have been the bright red flags in troubled relationships. It is helpful to view money misuse initially as a problem that must be addressed and treated in its own right, with its own predictable pattern and progression. The simultaneous challenge is to reach deeper and address underlying issues that are the soil in which obsession grows.

Society's Role

American society encourages compulsive spending and other money obsessions. In the last fifteen years, credit has been extended to people who never before had received such offers. Credit is no longer reserved for major appliances and paid off in full until the fridge conks out and a new loan is sought. Our economy is dependent on consumer debt. One needn't be an economist to realize that, without consumer debt, the nation's economy would nose-dive. Consider the recession of the early nineties, when Americans were encouraged to buy, buy, buy, for the sake of the economy. Our congressmen and women have done their part as well. In 1992, it was discovered that 296 members of the Congress had written bad checks at the House bank. Some representatives had written hundreds of checks with insufficient funds. When elected officials, one of whom chaired the House Ethics Committee, spend tomorrow's money today, it is an ominous sign of the times.

Most citizens are in no position to buy excessively, much less on credit and unearned income. Both personal bankruptcies and consumer debt have doubled in the last decade.[6] Consumer Credit Counseling Services has been opening an average of two new offices per week across the country.

Can't Buy Me Love results from a growing awareness of money traps and their tragic (and usually unspoken) consequences. The goal is to offer the reader new knowledge and tools for understanding the emotional landmines of overspending and other money obsessions.

Questionnaires will help readers to identify a money problem and then trace the progression backward to its seeds. *Can't Buy Me Love* describes the effects of money misuse on self-esteem as well as on relationships with others. Step-by-step solutions guide the reader through a recovery program. The book also presents a way to intervene and help others who have this problem as well as a guide to teaching money responsibility to children.

The authors hope that *Can't Buy Me Love* will be helpful to Clair and all of the other women and men like her who are in the grip of their personal money traps.

Sally Coleman
Nancy Hull-Mast

Part One

The Full Closet, Garage, Refrigerator, House

CHAPTER

1

The Plastic Placebo

Each year new wallets seem to have more slots in which to store credit cards. Wallet slots tell us a lot about what we value. Security, fun, safety, and status are all symbolic of the use of credit in America. For many, credit cards have become a soothing placebo and supposed tickets to instant happiness.

Like most everything else, credit or charge cards have a place and can be a positive thing. Used appropriately, they provide a service. They offer convenience without much additional expense, if they are paid in full each month, and they are effective record keeping devices with detailed statements sent to home or business. They provide a multitude of handy services and conveniences such as insurance plans, cash advances, buyer protection, and bonus incentives including reduced or free airfares.

People who are spending wisely and have money are using credit appropriately. In fact, most people who use credit or charge cards do so responsibly. This book, however, focuses on the dysfunctional use of money and spending that is out of control.

Although credit has been represented to American consumers as the route to security, fun, safety, and status, that promise is illusory. Daily advertisers bombard consumers with slogans and images promoting instant gratification that results in debt. Here are some examples: "One World One Card"—with the Berlin Wall down and the end of the cold war this slogan is undeniably politically correct. "Master the Possibilities"—most folks consider themselves masters of precious little, and this ad suggests an opportunity to be the master of something, albeit at eighteen or so percent interest. "You've Got the Option" appeals to people who feel they rarely get a say in anything. If they feel trapped in a situation and must struggle to get by, they might welcome the idea of having some options once in a while.

"Don't Leave Home without It" says another advertising slogan. Why? So in case you get into an accident the nurses in the hospital will know you have clean underwear and good credit? This ad implies that nobody is safe to leave home without a charge card. "Membership Has Its Privileges"—if you can't belong to a country club, at least you can be privileged with plastic. Master the Moment"—Carpe diem! It's a common fear that you may miss out on something that comes around only once in a lifetime. This slogan plays right into that fear. "It's Everywhere You Want to Be"—except that it doesn't entitle you to go where those tanned tourists hang out on TV. Most of us just can't afford to look conspiratorially at our partners, catch the next flight, and buy luggage and wardrobe when we get there. Lots of people are not where they want to be in life, and this ad campaign reminds them of that. Like all credit card ads, it's enticing, exciting, and seductive advertising.

Plastic Safety Nets

Americans have been conditioned by some of the most creative minds in the advertising industry to believe that credit cards are like seat belts, oat bran, sex, and aspirin all rolled into one convenient ready-to-use package; they protect, nourish, feel great, and cure pain. The drama portrayed on television for credit cards looks so exciting. American Express shows the world traveler being greeted warmly and cheerfully everywhere he goes. This ad aims at our need for a sense of belonging and acceptance. Visa shows someone in a personal crisis who is bailed out with a credit card. The rescue plays well with our need to feel safe and protected by someone or something beyond ourselves. Some ads suggest that teens and young adults need charge cards. These appeals effectively hook a parent's fear that the child may become involved in a crisis away from home when the parent is too far away to help.

Along with the professionally designed TV and radio spots and printed ads, Americans joke about their spending with phrases like "Shop till you drop," "I shop, therefore I am," and "When the going gets tough, the tough go shopping." As always, people reveal themselves in humor. These jests are just socially acceptable rationalizations to spend unearned income.

Americans even have products that promote shopping and charging. There are chocolate credit cards, a game for teenage girls called Mall-Madness, and special shopping shoes specifically designed to give comfort and support to the frequent shopper. Some Christmas ornaments resemble shoppers using credit cards, and T-shirts and sweatshirts say "I'd rather be shopping." It's no wonder spending and incurring debt has become a popular American pastime. To get the whole story, however, people need to put the glamour and sizzle aside and observe the reality of credit card use.

On TV these days, ads offer credit to anyone, regardless of credit history. This disregard of money problems implies "cheap grace" from the creditors, the promise that debtors can be loved even though they've been naughty. The announcer's conciliatory tone assures people that his company is not like the bully down the street who refused them credit. How ironic that the phone call made to this company is likely to cost between nine and thirty-five dollars, a cost suggesting the true nature of "easy credit."

So many people have abused credit that an entire industry has been created to serve them. The fierce grip of excessive spending causes people to jump into the fire over and over again, no matter how badly they have been burned before, because they can't face the fear of abstinence. If they took away the mask of spending, they might find unmet emotional needs that require attention, and this prospect can be terrifying. If their needs for affirmation, safety, love, security, acceptance, and self-esteem are not met, the distracting dysfunctional use of money can push these problems out of consciousness, at least temporarily. Tackling those unmet needs would involve pain, time, and struggle. Americans live, however, in a society that doesn't wait. We can't wait any longer to resolve painful emotional issues than we can for a hamburger and fries; quick solutions are the standard. If we have a headache, we pop a pill. If we're looking for a mate, we may use a dating service to save time. Modern American society is an automated, computerized, turbo-charged society, at the expense of the emotional health of its citizens.

Status Seduction

From the time a child is born, the label frenzy begins. There are chic designer strollers, bibs, bottles, layettes, pacifiers, booties, and just about everything made for babies. As they grow, parents buy them status bed sheets, pajamas, and toys. Ads remind us that children are young only once, so "Master the Moment." Birthday parties at home have given way to theme parties at restaurants with paid entertainment. Luaus, circuses, and Mexican fiestas are becoming the norm for three-year-olds with middle-income or upper-income parents. If children have seen it all by age twelve, what can they look forward to? They're picking up messages like these: money buys good birthdays; money buys the clothes they need to feel accepted; money hangs out with money; and if people don't have money, they should use credit cards so they can act as if they do.

These are very serious messages about what is valuable and what is not. Families that bow to the pressure incur debts in order to keep up; they set in motion a destructive pattern of spending unearned money. No one benefits when status becomes more important than one's self, but many make that choice just the same.

A woman we interviewed, Carol, told us she incurs debts in order to give gifts that are similar to those her friends give to her and her children. She lives in an affluent area where her friends can afford to do more than she can. She never says "I can't afford it." She just buys on credit. She admits that the pressure to keep up with the Joneses is self-imposed. "If I had ten dollars to my name and I needed groceries and the neighbor kid was having a birthday, not only would I use the money for the gift, I'd add another five to ten dollars for a more expensive present."

Carol is running fast but getting nowhere. She lives in fear that someday she will be exposed to her friends and neighbors for what she really is. She hasn't been true to herself for so long that she not only fears others' disapproval if they were to see the real Carol, but she's also afraid she wouldn't like what she found. Occasionally she day-dreams about moving the family to a farm, somewhere far away where no one owns a BMW or even wants one. Then she realizes she could never be that far from good shopping.

Americans commonly hold false beliefs about money. To illustrate these ideas, imagine a guy going into a bicycle shop and seeing a bike that he just can't pass up. It's on sale, but he doesn't have any money. I'll pay for it with my credit card, he thinks, but his conscience reminds him of the debt he already owes. I deserve it—I haven't bought anything for myself in ages, he thinks as he hands the card to the clerk.

False belief: *We can buy things without money.* No, we can't. Credit cards represent future income. Purchases made with credit cards cost an extra 11 to 21 percent in interest. Our culture has bought into the delusion that credit cards are what we should use when we can't afford something or don't yet have the money.

False belief: *If I deserve it now, I should buy it now.* Sometimes life isn't fair, however, and we can't always have what we feel we deserve. The following examples of Dan and Zoe exemplify the distortion of that fact.

Dan and his date were having dinner with two other couples at a restaurant. When the check arrived, Dan put the tab on his credit card, and the other couples paid him their share. After receiving their money, Dan had a wallet full of cash and he felt great, as if he had received something for nothing. Dan knew the bill would arrive in a few weeks, but at the moment, his emotional self felt rich. Dan spent the money long before his credit card bill came.

Zoe worked full-time to put herself through law school. It took a long, long time and required many sacrifices. When she finally passed the bar exam, Zoe wanted to celebrate. Her best friend, planning a two-week trip to Florida, invited Zoe to accompany her. Zoe's seven credit cards were at their limits, however, and she had several loans out already. With no cash on hand, she didn't know how she would pay this month's rent. But she longed to go! She felt she deserved it, had earned it, and was entitled to it. In a sense, she was right; she did deserve a reward. But the fact was, she didn't have the money. She couldn't afford the trip.

In making her decision, Zoe could focus all of her energy on the scarcity that would result from the lost opportunity to go to Florida, or she could focus on the future abundance and health that would result from her declining the invitation. Her occupation should provide her with endless opportunities to build wealth, earn money, and get the most pleasure from life. She could choose health and work her way out of debt, consequently finding abundance in herself as well as her bank book. Or, impelled by her money obsession, she could decide that she deserved that trip and could beg, borrow, or steal to get it. That decision, however, would just bring her more debt and more frustration at her inability to afford what she "deserves."

False belief: *Every sale is an opportunity, even f we don't have any money.* Using a sale as an excuse to shop is a way to rationalize possible compulsive behavior. What is saved in a sale purchase is often lost in credit card interest.

Many sales are teasers to lure the shopper, who nibbles the bait and then is enticed to buy non-sale items. The device of a sale tempts shoppers into unplanned purchases, which often are unnecessary and unaffordable.

Shelby read an ad in the paper about an annual sale of designer shoes and handbags at an expensive department store. Ordinarily she avoided the place because the prices were too high, but the sale drew her in. At lunch hour, when her coworkers headed for nearby restaurants, Shelby was hot on the trail of Picone, Vuitton, Klein, and Claiborne. She discovered that all of the sale items were unusual things in very small or very large sizes. She bought a standard-size purse, not a sale item, and rationalized her decision because it was cheaper than other purses at regular price in that store, ignoring the fact that it was still too expensive. When she returned to the office, she told her associates that she had gone to a sale at the expensive store and bought a purse. The next day, two others from her office also went to the sale.

People need to realize that they can't buy things without money. They can't always have what they deserve, and sale purchases don't pay for themselves no matter how large the discount. Acceptance of these truths is essential to healthy spending.

Healthy Spending versus Unhealthy Spending

The philosophy expressed in Debtor's Anonymous (DA) literature (see the recommended reading list at the back of the book) dovetails with the personal life experiences and familiar themes described by spenders who are in therapy. Compulsive spending differs from healthy spending in that it becomes an obsession and eventually a compulsion that takes control of a person's life. *Obsessions* are persistent, all-consuming ideas or impulses. *Compulsions* are repetitive actions performed in response to obsessions. These compulsive actions cover up and temporarily soothe deeper powerful anxieties or other life problems. When compulsive acts become habitual and cyclical, they are difficult to stop, and resistance may produce tension. This tension then eases temporarily when a person says "Oh, what the heck" and gives in to the compulsion.

Obsessive-compulsive spending behavior distracts money misusers, thereby masking deeper life problems and fears and keeping them at a distance. Compulsions can be viewed as valuable markers of deeper issues and needs, perhaps including a biochemical imbalance requiring medical assessment as part of a complete emotional health treatment plan. A pattern of compulsive money misuse is a red flag that creates an opportunity to examine and discover painful feelings and life events that have been lost, ignored, or pushed away. A compulsion in fact challenges the quality of life and begs to be seen as a window into real life pain that needs to be healed.

Healthy spenders *choose* to spend, but compulsive spenders *must* spend. The problem progresses through three basic stages: warning, loss of control, and deterioration. Compulsive spending springs from emotional losses and feelings of deprivation. Initially money may be used to relieve and soothe painful feelings such as low self-esteem, inadequacy, and boredom, or as a way to celebrate successes. If a little spending feels good, then more spending feels better. Sooner or later, unchecked compulsive spending changes from a soothing "friend" to a disruptive and all-consuming enemy. Spending more and more in hopes of getting good feelings becomes a full-time job. Once spenders lose control of their spending, they become caught in a vicious cycle of wanting to stop the pain but feeling obsessed and then compelled to spend. Compulsive spending in the deterioration phase affects every area of the spender's life.

Obsessions and compulsions are what *Can't Buy Me Love* is all about. As you read Ginny's story in the next chapter you will better understand the life of a compulsive spender and be able to see how it differs from the life of someone who can use money as one component in a healthy, happy life.

CHAPTER

2

Ginny's Story

You'd think she was in her twenties. Ginny's small frame and long, wavy hair take at least ten years off her actual age of thirty-seven. Even when she had her two small children in the shopping cart, the clerk asked Ginny for identification when she purchased beer or wine with groceries. She didn't take it as a compliment, however. Looking young felt to her like one more thing to overcome. It made her feel that she wasn't taken seriously, as if she were an impostor living among adults. Ginny felt mature and important only when she shopped.

Spending money gave her temporary feelings of power, authority, and strength. Before a shopping trip, Ginny was preoccupied but calm. She knew she would be spending soon, so nothing really upset her. Her head swam with anticipation and excitement, but she remained unflappable on the exterior. Just knowing that she was about to spend produced a feeling almost as intense as the actual shopping.

Sometimes Ginny shopped with her children. If she had an urge to spend, it didn't matter whether her children needed their naps or hadn't had lunch yet. Her impulse to spend was so strong that it sometimes overpowered her sense of responsibility as a mother. Once she took her children shopping at a mall when she knew her daughter wasn't feeling well. Standing in line, waiting to pay for some clothes, the girl vomited. After the mess was cleaned up and the spectators went back to their own shopping, Ginny's mind played tricks on her. She considered going home to care for her child. Then she thought she might as well finish what she had started, thereby eliminating the need to return to the store and start over. She came to believe that she actually was doing something positive for the child, who usually enjoyed their shopping sprees.

Ginny did not take her children on the better-organized shopping trips but usually hired a baby sitter. These "big" days were well thought out. Ginny pored over the credit card bills, trying to figure out whether she had used up her credit limit. She wrote all of the information down: twenty-five dollars left on Visa, one hundred dollars on MasterCard. Since she and her husband Noel had six bank cards, eight department store cards, and two American Express cards, the calculations were a tedious process. Ginny had two additional secret bank cards in her name.

Ginny's other financial deceptions included the use of cash advances from new credit cards to pay the minimum balance on the existing cards. To delay paying American Express, she once called the company and told them they had made a terrible mistake: "I charged ten times the amount you've billed me for! I'll just hold onto the bill and wait until you locate the errors. I certainly wouldn't want someone else being billed for my purchases." She deftly handled the confused representative on the other end of the line and bought herself some time.

The closer her big spending binges were, the more confused her thoughts. As she drove toward the store, her thinking became more frantic and disjointed. Her head swam with thoughts like, I should get the car washed. It'll only take a minute. . . . No! I want to go straight to the mall. I don't want to make any stops. Now, I have to think—I'm almost there, so I have to think this thing out. Okay, okay, first Visa, MasterCard, Field's, Carson's, Neiman's, Saks those are all up to the limit, but if I pay the minimum on one of the Visas for one more month, they'll up my limit and then I can get a cash advance to pay Bloomingdale's, which is now ninety days past due. And even though I'll be used up on *that* Visa, I might have something left on the other one by then. I cannot understand why Jeremy doesn't like barbecued chicken, but the really good sales are at Mathon's. . . . Transitions between thoughts were disorderly. Ginny felt the anticipation and suspense of a child getting ready to go out and play. It was rejuvenating, an adult fix.

Even before the spending bout began, Ginny set up her excuses. Noel was an alcoholic, and Ginny perceived him as cold and arrogant. She described their relationship as analogous to a parent-child struggle. The more she struggled for praise, affection, and recognition the more she felt dismissed by a withholding parent. She justified her spending, believing she was doing it *in response* to Noel; if he would change, she explained to herself, she wouldn't be so lonely and need to spend so much money. This line of reasoning worked especially well just after a fight.

In the stores Ginny felt at home. She felt safe. Whenever she shopped, she thought of the movie *Breakfast at Tiffany's*, in which Audrey Hepburn says that the jewelry store is her favorite place because "nothing bad can happen to you at Tiffany's." Ginny knew exactly what that meant. To her, a store was a safe and beautiful place. Its scents were sensual. Cologne, shoe leather, freshly cut and stitched fabrics, candy, and the combined scents of other shoppers, seduced her senses.

The more purchases Ginny made, the more daring she became. She started using credit cards she knew were not on her list. Often the sales clerk told her the card had been declined, but Ginny had long since ceased to be embarrassed about that. When she ran out of credit, she wrote checks. When she ran out of money in her checking account, she wrote bad checks, certain she could figure out a way to cover them before the bank called.

At home, after a bout of spending, Ginny felt good for a while— a very short while. Then the feelings of guilt, remorse, and intense anxiety surfaced. The experience was never as fulfilling as she had planned. An emptiness, a loneliness returned as she secretly removed the store tags, scuffed up her new shoes, and went about hiding some of her purchases and putting others away. Ginny was methodical in covering up. She had convinced Noel so many times that new clothes were actually old or gifts that sometimes she came to believe it herself.

(To be continued in part II.)

3

Compulsive Spending Survey

People who are caught in compulsions have difficulty changing their behavior partly because they cannot distance themselves sufficiently to see their actions clearly. The purpose of this chapter is to provide that detachment. The Compulsive Spending Survey will help you to assess your own specific spending patterns. Maintain a willing, open mind as you begin to analyze your behavior. The survey asks very specific questions to aid your developing a personal spending profile. Circle any of the numbers that apply to your spending behaviors and attitudes. Answer quickly, recording your first response.

1. Spending helps me forget my troubles.
2. I feel more alive when I buy something.
3. More than once I've thought, Today is the last time I'll overspend. I'll start a budget tomorrow.
4. The anticipation of a spending trip is an exhilarating high.
5. I can count on spending and shopping not to let me down. I feel good when I spend money.
6. Spending and thinking about spending eases my loneliness.
7. Spending is one of the best things I can do to relieve boredom.
8. "This was the best deal of the year and I couldn't pass it up" is a statement I frequently make to myself and others.
9. When I go on a diet or quit drinking, I spend more.
10. I have made resolutions and promises to change the ways I spend money.
11. After a fight with a loved one, I spend more.

12. When I feel bad about myself, I spend more.
13. When I feel happy, I often celebrate by spending.
14. I feel happier going to stores than I do going almost anywhere else.
15. I work hard, so I deserve to relax and shop on days off.
16. I feel less guilty when I overspend on food, because food is necessary.
17. It feels good to look into a full closet, garage, and workshop.
18. I don't like to share information about sales until after I've gone shopping.
19. I feel like a good person when I get a bargain.
20. I feel elated when I return something I bought.
21. I opened a new credit card account because the old one was at its limit.
22. Creditors are sending me overdue notices.
23. I have begun to write checks with no money in my account, planning that my next deposit will cover them.
24. Sometimes I feel guilty, nervous, and irritable after spending.
25. I have begun to be late in paying my rent and utilities.
26. I'm especially nice to others after I spend money.
27. My loved one and I often argue about money.
28. When I overspend, I often convince myself that something will happen to bail me out.
29. I buy gifts because I believe the receiver will like me more.
30. I sometimes postdate checks so payments won't bounce.
31. I no longer have a savings account.
32. I've borrowed money to pay for regular household expenses such as rent, food, clothing, and insurance.
33. I'm not sure exactly how much installment debt I have.
34. I feel a tremendous relief when I'm approved for a loan.
35. I rarely buy personal items for myself, but I go to the grocery store and binge spend on items I don't need or won't use.
36. I live on the edge of my credit power and fear monthly statements.
37. I always find something wrong in an item, so I return it.

38. When I think about the fun I had on vacations, I remember the places I shopped.
39. I can overspend, but I get angry when others in my family do the same.
40. I get defensive when asked about my spending habits.
41. Confronted about overspending, I promise myself and others never to do it again. I sincerely believe I will keep my promises.
42. My personality changes before, during, and after a spending period.
43. Sometimes I quit spending or limit my spending to prove to myself and others that I don't have a problem.
44. In an attempt to control my spending, I've switched stores and tried to change my habits and patterns.
45. I missed work to shop and spend.
46. I have had a credit card revoked.
47. I regularly check my mailbox hoping to receive some unexpected money.
48. I promised payment to creditors and then didn't fulfill my promise.
49. I have given new items away because I felt too guilty to bring them home.
50. I spend a lot of my time worrying about money.
51. After spending too much, I easily forget how bad I felt afterward by remembering only the fun and excitement of buying.
52. The worst part of my day is the time when the stores are closed.
53. When bills arrive that I can't pay, I sometimes go out and spend some more.
54. I feel that I could never have too many shoes, purses, and other special merchandise.
55. I wouldn't consider living anywhere that wasn't close to good shopping—lots of different kinds of stores.
56. Shopping and overspending is becoming my secret life.
57. I increasingly lie and break promises to myself and others about spending.
58. I feel that I might spend less if I moved to a new location.
59. I consolidated my debts only to go into debt again.

60. I tore up credit cards and closed bank accounts, but I still find ways to overspend.
61. Spending and money problems are making my life unmanageable.
62. Overspending causes me to neglect my family's needs.
63. I sometimes have memory loss when spending.
64. I now need to spend more than I used to in order to feel good.
65. I am never ready happy with the way I look, and I constantly plan to buy something that will make me look better.
66. I regularly deprive myself in order to give special gifts to others.
67. I know that something is wrong with my spending, but I feel powerless to stop.
68. I hide my purchases in the garage, basement, car trunk, or other safe places after spending.
69. I think that some clerks know I can't afford to spend money.
70. I scuff up new shoes and wash new clothes so they won't look new to others.
71. If buying one sweater makes me feel good, buying five will make me feel great.
72. I frequently return things to relieve my guilt.
73. Every day I hope I find the perfect object to buy.
74. When another person is with me, I act uninterested and don't spend money as I would if I were alone.
75. I've stopped shopping with friends because they hamper my spending style.
76. I panic when I think I can't buy something I want.
77. I hate the way the merchandise looks when I see it at home.
78. I feel ashamed when I overspend.
79. Sometimes I bribe and threaten my children not to tell my spouse about my spending.
80. I regularly skip meals in order to shop.
81. I panic when thinking about a vacation in a remote area with nowhere to shop.
82. I sometimes feel lightheaded and disoriented during a spending trip.

83. I rationalize my overspending by saying everyone else does it.
84. I follow people in stores who have something I want, hoping they'll put it back so I can buy it.
85. I often lose all sense of time when I spend.
86. When I start spending, I can't predict how or when I'll stop.
87. Once I buy the first item, I feel powerless to stop spending until I am exhausted or the stores close.
88. The best thing about Thanksgiving and Christmas are the special shopping days that follow.
89. I tore up my credit cards but recorded the numbers so I can still use them for mail or phone orders.
90. I borrowed money to pay off my credit cards but resisted closing the accounts.
91. I no longer carry my credit cards, but I have the clerks call for authorization when I find something I like.
92. I regularly overspend on my American Express card. That one is different because I have to pay it off each month.
93. After spending money, I relax, unwind, and soothe myself with drinks or a special meal.
94. I take a tranquilizer or drink before shopping because my spending makes me nervous.
95. I am often too tired to have sex after a big spending day.
96. I would rather spend money than talk, have sex, go to a movie, read a book, or do anything else.
97. My family and friends complain about my spending.
98. I sold treasured possessions to pay debts.
99. I defrauded insurance companies to get cash.
100. I took cash advances on one credit card to pay the minimum balance on another.
101. My sleep patterns have been severely disrupted because of my spending worries.
102. I neglected my work, family, and other personal responsibilities for days at a time because of my spending patterns and financial difficulties.
103. In a panic, I attempted to find creditors who would lend me money.

104. After spending, I have had severe bouts with depression, anxiety, or physical illness.
105. When I don't have money, I shoplift.
106. My spending secrets are too shameful to tell anyone.
107. I make a decent salary, yet my gas, electricity, telephone, or other utility has been cut off for nonpayment.
108. I declared bankruptcy due to my spending behaviors.
109. I am divorced because of my spending behaviors.
110. I lost my home because of my overspending.
111. I feel compelled to shop and spend.
112. I stole money from my family, friends, and others to cover my spending excesses.
113. I borrowed large sums of money from my family and friends and didn't pay them back.
114. I embezzled money from my employer.
115. I attempted or seriously considered suicide as a result of my money worries.
116. I feel chronically tired and depressed because of money worries.
117. I feel angry when anyone questions me about money.
118. I spend as an alcoholic drinks.
119. I incurred attorney's costs because of my spending.
120. I was prosecuted for a crime because of my spending.
121. I have been barred from having a checking account because of my spending.
122. I was barred from stores because of my spending.
123. Someone gave me this book, or I bought this book, because of concern about my spending.

Scoring

Phase One

Chapter 5 explains the progression of compulsive spending through stages. Yes answers to questions 1-25 above especially indicate that you may be in an early stage. This phase is characterized by a developing pattern of spending for relief of tension and mood elevation as well. These signs are early indications that negative life consequences are emerging. Consider yes answers in this section of the survey to be early warning signs.

Phase Two

Yes answers to questions 26-95 especially indicate involvement in the middle stage of compulsive spending. The loss of control is marked by a pattern of inability to plan spending consistently. Secrets, lies, mood swings, and relationship disruptions indicate a problem. Yes answers here are evidence of the loss-of-control phase.

Phase Three

Yes answers to questions 96-124 especially indicate possible involvement in a late stage of compulsive spending. Deterioration is characterized by severe losses and destructive consequences in major life areas. Fears, dread, isolation, and despair run rampant as self-esteem and relationships collapse.

CHAPTER

4

Getting to Know More about Yourself

As people begin to inventory their behavior, styles, and attitudes about money, spending, and debt, they need an honest, open mind. As their vision about money expands, they will begin to understand the ways in which they or someone they love may be harmfully involved with compulsive spending, excessive debt, or other money abuses. Exploration of past and present relationships reveal effects on current actions and values regarding money. The more willing they are to review their history and the emotional components of money use, the greater will be their growth. Honesty about money may be a new and challenging experience for many. People who first begin to unravel their money history are often surprised by the confusion and clutter they find. As they dig deeper into the past, they may be shocked to discover how tightly their current money problems and patterns are woven with their childhood experiences. Present spending styles and patterns are often a tangible reflection of childhood losses and other early life experiences.

We have found it very helpful to begin raising our money awareness by identifying and reviewing our own spending styles. Personalize this book by writing in it. Freely record similarities and points that otherwise relate to you, as you answer questions and take stock.

Spending Styles

We all have different and unique personalities; individual differences are apparent in the way we spend money. Read through the following spending styles and see whether one or more describe your spending patterns. Few people fit exactly into one particular style, but many can identify with several of the spending patterns. Honestly acknowledging your own habits will lay the groundwork for understanding the ways you use money and the consequences it has in your life.

Returners

Returners are "hooked" in the obsessive and consuming decision-making process that follows the buy. After a shopping spree, they become obsessed with the rightness or wrongness of their purchase. They agonize, plagued by guilt and spinning thoughts, until they finally decide to return their purchases. They may stack or lay out the items in their homes as they vacillate about returning them. Home decor changes often as they display new items for short periods of time. A different lamp may appear every few weeks; closets fill up and empty out as purchases are juggled, hidden, or moved around before their return.

Erratic emotional highs and lows characterize the lives of compulsive returners. The act of making a purchase is very enjoyable. It feels a bit dangerous but just enough to be exciting and fun. Sometimes after the purchase, feelings of remorse, fear, and guilt take over. Then comes the agonizing about whether to return the item. Often these shoppers are mortified when they return the goods, especially if they have a history of shopping and returning at that store. One woman had several different colored wigs that she wore to disguise herself because she dreaded being recognized by clerks. Her suspicion that the clerk knew her secret life created panic and feelings of shame. She always felt great relief after she completed a return.

Time usually elapses between returners' shopping sprees, while the memory of previous incidents' unpleasantness gradually fades. The onset of a new episode is signaled by growing feelings of restlessness, anxiety, and fantasizing about shopping. The excitement of the binge temporarily relieves this discomfort. Some returners are in financial trouble and can't afford to buy anything new. Hooked on spending, however, they continue to buy. They return merchandise, much as a bulimic vomits food, trying after the fact to gain control of uncontrollable behavior and to avoid additional financial stress.

Sadly, many compulsive spenders become so obsessed with returning purchases that they find it difficult to shop and keep what they buy, even if it is affordable and needed. Some people who are financially able to buy feel unworthy of ownership. Nevertheless driven, they use shopping and returning as a form of self-punishment and deprivation. They equate owning nice things with saying the impossible: I am not a victim; I am worthwhile. Feelings of shame and unworthiness must be acknowledged, grieved, and healed before these returners can buy things and use them with pleasure.

Specialty Buyers

People who compulsively buy specialty merchandise search desperately for the perfect purchase. Feeling that they best can justify spending money if they make the "right purchase," they go to extraordinary lengths to find the highest quality or most unique item. This activity may take days, weeks, or months; by the time these people make the purchase, the joy feels distant, and the item usually doesn't satisfy them. Homes of specialty buyers are filled with large assortments of items that don't fit in or go together. A living room may contain five different clocks even though the owner doesn't collect clocks. Rooms may be cluttered. More often items are meticulously displayed. These homes may seem thrown together in a random order, like showrooms rather than comfortable havens. A man we know expanded his garage twice to accommodate the clutter of antique tools he had collected even though he wasn't a handyman. His car stereo was stolen three times before he rearranged his tools to make room for his car.

Some specialty buyers focus on certain items and buy them compulsively. After the items are purchased, they fall into the family of like items. Collectors behave differently than specialty buyers because they treat their collections with pride and care and seem to have a sense of balance and planning in their purchasing and arranging. Specialty buyers may lose interest shortly after their purchase is made and begin a new search for more perfect things.

Binge Spenders

Some shoppers take the bingeing character of their compulsive shopping to a greater extreme than others. Because they feel great remorse and regret after overspending, they usually make strong resolutions to keep their spending under control. Even more than others who abuse money, they have a need to spend that seems to have a life of its own. After a period of guilt-free fiscal responsibility, they go on a spending spree. They fall deeper into debt and may begin returning goods in order to continue their habit.

These addicts experience an emotional roller coaster ride. Excitement builds before a spree, quickly accelerating once they have made the decision to spend. Then they develop a consuming, single-minded focus to spend as quickly as possible. They change social arrangements or work plans with little concern for the feelings of others. A worker might miss a major sales meeting because she lost track of time during a lunch hour shopping spree. She eventually might lose her job because of her inability to return to work in time once she stepped onto the treadmill of her compulsion. Spree spenders often seem anxious and scatterbrained to others. Their clothing and homes may reflect their compulsive and hurried styles. Rooms may be cluttered and closets jammed with impulsive purchases. After the emotional and physical experience of a spending spree, these people feel exhausted to the point of near collapse. Waves of guilt soon follow the exhaustion as the reality of their spree sets in: Why did I buy a new TV when the old one was perfectly good? How will I pay next month's credit card bill? Gradually they rationalize remorse away. As guilt fades, the need to spend becomes increasingly powerful. Eventually they repeat the pattern.

Catalog Shoppers

Catalog shoppers are on every conceivable mailing list. Their mailboxes often cannot hold the weight and bulk of the many catalogs delivered daily to their homes. They may have catalogs in almost every room of the house. Catalogs usually take priority over the newspaper, books, and magazines. One woman developed an elaborate filing system for her catalogs that eventually took over her TV room; her family watched TV in the basement when her catalogs crowded them out. Her only complaint was that she didn't have enough time in her day to read her catalogs.

These shoppers spend so much time poring over their catalogs that they neglect responsibilities at home and work. They become transfixed by the photographs of lawn and garden accessories, designer clothing, children's toys, linens, home appliances, small gadgets, or whatnots. Since many catalogs offer twenty-four-hour phone service for placing orders, the looking, ordering, and sometimes returning is a round-the-clock practice for a great many catalog shoppers.

When the packages arrive, so do wonder and excitement. Almost everyone loves to receive "brown paper packages tied up with string." But along with the packages and warm feelings come the bills; often the purchaser cannot afford the merchandise. When the shopper confronts the ever-growing credit card balances and overdue notices, remorse and shame set in.

TV Shoppers

These people use home shopping programs to satisfy their need to spend. They may become so obsessed with finding the right purchase that they feel uncomfortable when the TV is off. From early morning to late at night, they watch and wait for the right item. We have talked with people who have become enraged with spouses, more interested in bargains than sex, who refused to turn off the shopping channel when they made love. Eventually these shoppers may find it hard to take time to clean, prepare meals, and go out, lest they miss the right purchase. The life of a person whose TV shopping is out of control revolves around the television schedule. Buyers often become emotionally connected to the host of the shopping program and delight in hearing their names broadcast, thrilled to have pleased the host. This superficial relationship is a compelling and seductive ingredient of TV shopping.

Such a shopper takes over the family room. A well-worn, comfortable arm chair is usually positioned near a snack table that holds paper, pens, and a telephone. The room is arranged for focused viewing. Since shoppers may become irritated and angry when someone wants to talk or change the channel, their homes often contain two TVs, one for the entertainment of others and one for shopping.

Credit Card Collectors

Credit card collectors are emotionally involved with the power of plastic. Nothing feels better than flashing a wallet full of these licenses to buy. The thought of losing or destroying credit cards creates feelings of panic, since these people associate their cards with safety; they serve as a subconscious extension of the self. Therefore, card collectors exert every effort to maintain their privileges. They take impulsive trips and go on prolonged spending sprees, but when they have reached their credit limit, they juggle almost anything to keep their cards.

A real estate broker talked with us about what she called her greatest professional fear. She was terrified that she would be without her credit cards and unable to rent a car when she traveled. She had lost two businesses in two years because of her mismanagement but refused to acknowledge that her money excesses had contributed to these disasters. Buying has gone haywire when the credit card holder no longer can manage the monthly balancing act. This crisis often is signaled by the use of cash advances from one card to pay the minimum amount on another. Some people have hocked family heirlooms and sold their homes and cars in order to keep their beloved cards; revocation would mean a symbolic loss of self.

Credit card collectors may develop secret lives to hide their spending. They feel controlled by daily mail delivery, compelled to intercept their bills before anyone else sees them. They even have bills sent to the homes of friends or to post office boxes.

Just Lookers

Just lookers find it almost impossible to buy anything, but they nevertheless become obsessed with shopping. Most of their waking hours are spent thinking about their next shopping trip. They buy several different papers and pore over the ads, fantasizing about how they would dress or rearrange their homes with new purchases. Even if they have money, however, they stop short of a purchase, feeling an unrealistic, consuming guilt about spending.

Window shopping without buying is healthy recreation for many people. Problems occur when a shopper focuses obsessively on the shopping experience. Forced by necessity to purchase something, just lookers don't enjoy the experience. They feel burdened by the ownership of material possessions. Their homes and dress are simple, even drab and dreary. Just lookers live in a fantasy world of what could be instead of what actually is.

Coupon Clippers and Refund Specialists

These shoppers spend large amounts of time collecting coupons and refunding, focused on how much money they are saving. This focus is the difference between a healthy habit and a compulsion. Problems develop when coupons become a central life focus that causes neglect of other relationships, responsibilities, and interests. Coupon clippers may become obsessed and preoccupied with finding all of the right coupons and refund slips. They subscribe to refund magazines, several newspapers, and other periodicals, devoting hours to them. Shopping trips and mail deliveries are the highlights of the week, overshadowing all other activities and interactions. One of our sources was ashamed to tell anyone that she relaxed the most when she was clipping and organizing her coupons. Although she rarely shopped with them, she felt anxious and uncomfortable if she didn't spend one or two hours sorting her collection each day.

Coupon clippers and refund specialists do save money, but at great cost of time and relationships with others. The problem may be difficult to recognize because the focus is on economy. Compulsive coupon clipping can take over refunders' homes, however. The kitchen table and counters are cluttered with magazines, coupons, and mail in the shoppers' urgency to save every cent possible. These compulsive shoppers may neglect nutritional needs and deprive themselves of necessities if coupons are not available. They may commit mail fraud, knowingly or not. Confiscating coupons from neighbors and friends, sending for refunds under assumed names, using another shopper's proof of purchase labels for rebates—these are only a few of the activities that may result in prosecution. In fact, many clippers have been prosecuted.

Sale Addicts

These people plan their leisure time around garage sales, thrift shops, flea markets, auctions, and department store clearances. Pursuit of a bargain becomes more important than need. Garages, closets, and basements often brim with cases of toilet paper, toothpaste, and other merchandise. Sale addicts sometimes build additional storage space; when their freezers are overflowing, they buy new freezers. They pride themselves on never running out of anything and being prepared for all emergencies.

The conversation of people who live for a sale centers, of course, on savings. They so love to parade their bargains that they seldom talk about a new chair or new tie without including the sale price. The bargain justifies their compulsive spending behavior. Unused and unopened items clutter their homes, items purchased for price, not for style and suitability. Monica and her single, middle-aged daughter Shirley proudly called themselves "sale freaks." They spent the majority of their leisure time running from clearance to clearance. After they returned home they engaged in a ritual they called 'The Showing," each laying out and arranging all of her purchases on the dining room table to show the other. They talked about these "showings" as some of the best memories they had of their relationship.

These compulsive spenders often get the jitters before and during a sale, desperately wishing to buy before anyone else. Exhaustion follows, along with feelings of emptiness and discontent. Sale addicts hate to hear about others' bargains, feeling cheated and personally affronted when they miss out on a good bargain. They sometimes criticize the purchases of others in order to feel wise and good about themselves.

Tag Tuckers

Some shoppers buy clothing, wear it, and then return it. They tuck the price tag up a sleeve so it won't show or take it off and say they never wore the item. This practice can backfire, as it did for a woman who told us about a day of horror. While she was giving a speech at her twentieth high school reunion, her suit tag waved in the breeze when she raised her hand to take a drink of water. Although she was deeply ashamed, she continued to return clothing she had worn.

Tag tuckers may buy different styles and sizes and wear them all before deciding which item to keep or return. They are satisfied by the experience of using the item and getting their money back. If forced to keep an item, they feel outraged. Tag tuckers feel they deserve to have what they want, especially if they can't afford it. They may become experts at steaming off and reattaching tickets. They may switch tags in order to keep an expensive item and return a cheaper one. They invent elaborate excuses to explain missing sale tags and receipts and may keep merchandise for long periods before returning it, savoring their feelings of ownership, power, and cleverness. Tag tuckers who charge their purchases often are forced to return items before the monthly bill arrives because of their inability to pay.

Most tag tuckers don't consider their behavior fraudulent, but it is. They rationalize their cheating by thinking of it as a "service" they receive from a store, a service to which they feel entitled because they are generally "good customers." Prices are too high, they tell themselves, and therefore force people to fight back. They believe they have no other option.

Smugglers

Compulsive shoppers may cover their shopping tracks when everyone else is away, sleeping, or in other parts of the house. They cut off tags, hide bags, scuff new shoes, and rearrange closets. After a shopping spree, they can't sleep or relax comfortably until their purchases are put away and the evidence hidden. Their guilt about money abuse causes them to sneak around and stash things in the garage, basement, or the trunk of a car until the coast is clear. It often feels safer to wait until everyone is asleep before retrieving the hidden items.

A man told us that he bribed his son into silence with a twenty-dollar bill when the boy found him sneaking two new drills into the garage at three o'clock in the morning. Smugglers' sleep patterns may be interrupted when they lie awake and worry until the evidence is safely put away. The sense of danger creates an experience that is difficult to interrupt.

Gift Buyers

Some people can shop for others, and even feel loved when they do so, but have more difficulty buying for themselves. Their seeming generosity makes compulsive spending more acceptable, but they are covering up their compulsion with self-deprivation. They feel that their needs are not important and do without in order to buy gifts for others. The recipients function as stand-ins or proxies for the buyer, who enjoys the gifts vicariously.

These spenders experience mounting anxiety as birthdays, holidays, and other special occasions approach. They feel obligated to give abundantly to others. If they don't have enough money for the perfect gift, they panic and extend credit or borrow money to keep up their spending habits.

Compulsive gift buyers delight in discovering the perfect item to buy for someone else. They often carry a mental shopping list in their heads of all the purchases they want to make for others. The may feel crushed when someone doesn't like a gift as much as they had hoped, but usually they recover quickly and continue their search. They cannot acknowledge that they have a problem because they see their desire to please others as noble and more important than caring for themselves. Spending on others is dysfunctional when it is done at the expense of the buyer's needs, or when buying for others creates unhealthy dependencies, becomes compulsive and obsessive, and causes financial stress.

Big Holiday Spenders

Some people get themselves into financial trouble annually by overspending at Christmas, Hanukkah, birthdays, Mother's Day and Father's Day, graduations, weddings, or any other holiday and special event. These compulsive spenders buy as if every special occasion were their last. They may plan for months in advance or go on a last minute shopping spree. Recipients feel confused and embarrassed by the excess, but the Santa Clauses become known for their lavish gifts and feel obliged to keep up the tradition. They may try to outdo themselves each year with even bigger and better packages. The big spenders often are agitated during holiday seasons and are difficult to be around. After the big day passes, they experience an empty feeling of incompleteness and dissatisfaction. Their lavish gift giving never produces the feelings they crave: affirmation, acceptance, love, and self-value. Lacking self-esteem, they cannot freely buy for their own needs. Holiday bills also contribute to the postholiday blues.

Guilt Inducers

Some compulsive money abusers overspend on gifts but always tell the beneficiaries the cost and sacrifice. They use buying to keep others financially and emotionally dependent on them, suggesting that the recipients are neither worthy to receive the gift nor sufficiently grateful. Consequently, their pleasure in receiving the gift is mixed with rage and depression about the emotional price tag. Guilt inducers are often emotionally changeable and may vacillate from loving to blaming. They usually have high expectations for themselves and others and may be plagued by irrational money worries.

These manipulative donors may initially want to give a nice gift to a special person, but they experience regret and anger after purchasing the gift. They may feel it costs too much money or suddenly may decide that the person doesn't deserve such a nice present. They seem to keep a running tally sheet in their heads in which they continuously tabulate the reactions and appreciation level as well as the current characteristics of significant others. Their gifts always have a hidden cost in self-esteem, and they pull these strings for years. One adult man still remembers, decades later, the sick feeling in the pit of his stomach whenever his dad came home from work with a package under his arm. He brought gifts for his wife on days he was especially mad at her. Instead of talking about the real reasons for his anger, he gave her gifts and then spent the evening in a tirade about his family's lack of appreciation for all that he did.

Guilt inducers sense resentment but don't understand its sources. These spenders are usually lonely people with long-term unmet needs who compulsively try to buy love and acceptance; at the same time, they push others away with their blaming and angry attitudes.

Suicidal Spenders

Money abuse often becomes so unmanageable that addicts exhibit stress related physical and emotional symptoms. These people may be committing emotional suicide in a relationship, unnecessarily forcing its end without confronting the underlying problems. The unexpressed anger that fuels a suicidal spender's behavior usually indicates a need for professional help and support. The rage may be so well hidden in a gift that others don't detect it, as it was when a man bought his wife an expensive red car, knowing that she hated that color. Not knowing or understanding the depth of their rage, suicidal spenders unwittingly overspend to get even with others.

Suicidal spenders often go on gigantic sprees that are disproportionate to their financial reality or the needs of others. They may be so caught up in their compulsion that they are oblivious to the consequences until their world crashes down. Backed into a financial corner, they feel sickened and hopeless and may reach such depths of depression that they consider suicide as a way out of their misery.

Maintenance Spenders

A compulsion may be difficult to identify if spending is subtle. Maintenance spenders must buy something almost every day, but the purchase need not be large or expensive; it might be only a lipstick or a screwdriver, but the buyer feels greatly relieved after spending the money. Maintenance spenders carry out a pattern of regular shopping and spending as a way to relax. The rituals of looking and choosing are the highlight of each day. A man might be unable to pass the drugstore on his way home from work, for example, ritually stopping there to soothe his spirits, even if he bought only a pack of gum.

The buying patterns of maintenance spenders consume great amounts of time, a factor that causes them to neglect responsibilities to themselves and others. Shopping is an escape that maintenance spenders need regularly in order to relax and feel good. Lots of gadgets and small miscellaneous items are in their kitchens, garages, workshops, and purses.

Money Jugglers

Patterns of negative excitement keep money jugglers afloat as they move from crisis to crisis. They become obsessed with living in danger, keeping their heads just above water. They usually pay their bills, but they undergo trauma to do so and may delay sending checks for monthly bills even though they have money in the bank. Money jugglers flirt with financial ruin, riding a roaring wave of emotions, always finding new, more clever ways to bail themselves out. They are hooked on the cycle of overspending and scheming to get enough money to make up for the overspending. Though they continually promise to stop the compulsive behavior, they are uncomfortable with financial stability. A recovering money juggler once ran up a $2,000 bill on his American Express card just to challenge himself and see how he would pay it off in a month. Such people may purchase items they don't need or rarely use and often can't remember what they bought the day before.

These compulsive spenders are usually high-energy people who never seem to sit still and have a hard time living a balanced life. They create their own fast track of ups and downs. Asked what is the biggest ongoing worry in their lives, they often say it is money worries. Money jugglers often are autocratic about their preference for spending and managing their money, and they may become defensive if someone tries to advise them or in any other way threatens their relationship with money. Though usually very generous, they feel that others are insensitive to their financial worries.

Not surprisingly, money jugglers often are overextended in their credit obligations and may feel helplessly unable to change. Stress-related emotional and physical conditions may be rampant. These addicts to excitement become involved in negative and unproductive relationships that seem immutable to them. Money management and financial ups and downs are a defense against a clear view of their personal needs and dissatisfactions.

Layaway Stashers

The layaway system is a wise and helpful plan that benefits many people who could not otherwise manage the purchase of large items. The concept of making a down payment on an item and paying it off later is, if properly used, a boon. This kind of shopping becomes problematic when it is excessive and compulsive. Layaway stashers become frantically involved in the experience of making down payments on different items. They have every intention of paying off the lay away on time but are unable to come up with the remaining money in the period contracted for. To distract themselves from their deeper life problems, these spenders become involved in the fantasy of buying, juggling layaways at several different stores. A great amount of plotting and scheming goes into decisions about which item to pay on and which to neglect. Beating the layaway deadline becomes an all-consuming game made worse by other unhealthy money choices. Owning the item matters less than the experience of obsessing about payment.

Men and Compulsive Spending

Men and women share many basic compulsive spending attitudes and styles, but some characteristics are more frequent in male compulsive spenders. We want to make it clear that we have not found over-spending, underspending, and other obsessive money abuse patterns to be more characteristic of either gender. Both men and women react to their need for emotional soothing by developing behavior that ultimately brings more pain into their lives. Our culture has assigned the role of breadwinner to men and gatherer to women. This tradition has led to a distorted view of females as "mall queens" who "shop till they drop" and males as the ones who carry the bags and pay the bills. Our clinical observations and investigations have shown us that men and women sometimes have *different* money use patterns that are in fact *variations of a theme common to both genders*. In the lives of both women and men, money and its emotional uses cause life-disrupting problems.

Both men and women can have life-disrupting patterns of money misuse and experience a wide variety of the symptoms during all phases of the progressive disorder. The patterns described here, however, seem to be more common in men than women.

Special Needs

Men more than women seem to buy specialty items compulsively, focusing their spending in an obsession to acquire the "best" or all examples of a product or gadget. A pair of friends had breakfast every Saturday morning and ritually visited all of the hardware stores in town in hopes of "finding a tool we don't have." They traded catalogs and other information about tools. Their preoccupation became an obsession that absorbed most of their free time and created financial hardships for them and their families.

It is acceptable and even expected for men to spend money on electronic equipment and tire rims, so extreme behavior is more easily visible when purchases are things like diamonds and fine wine. Buying and enjoying such goods is not unhealthy in itself. Problems develop when acquisition becomes obsessive and compulsive, creates a financial problem, or interferes with personal relationships.

A compulsion is an irresistible impulse to perform an act. The involuntary expense of time and money in the search for unneeded or unaffordable possessions is not rational. The obsession for ownership precedes the compulsive action of purchasing it. Obsessions and compulsions act hand in hand to establish and perpetuate behaviors. Obsessive compulsive buying in reality distracts a person from life problems and fears.

Business Necessities

Some men spend compulsively on business activities and needs such as entertainment and clothes. They may become so focused on their work that they feel compelled to spend obsessively in order to make the right impression. They may feel especially justified to spend for the "power look."

Risks and Thrills

Men may involve themselves in high-risk purchases such as real estate, stocks, bonds, and commodities, spending compulsively while juggling financial deals. These money abusers are hard to identify when spending is their vocation. They lose or make fortunes in a day and even resort to illegal means to keep the deals profitable. Ivan Boesky and Michael Milken are recent examples. Balance is the missing component in the high-risk spender's impulsive lifestyle. Eventually their deals collapse, and they have to scramble to begin again. The energy and hope fade as the damages mount.

Home Is My Castle

Some men justify compulsive spending in the name of home improvement and family protection. New additions, workshops, pools, expansions, and other nonstop projects are always on the horizon. They continually run to the lumberyard and hardware store to buy supplies, meanwhile ignoring the debt and problems in family relationships. Since these men are "improving family life," onlookers and the spenders themselves cannot see that the obsessive pattern is problematic.

Hitting the Big One

The hope that they will hit the big one and earn or win all of the money they'll ever need obsesses some men. They spend enormous amounts of time, money, and energy pursuing the latest scheme or deal. The excitement of new enterprises dies down in the face of the real daily toil required to make a dream come true. These men fix their vision more on the scheme than on the work it demands, often becoming involved in lotteries and other gambling. Somehow spending money compulsively seems all right in the pursuit of the illusory big payoff. This type of spending may escalate into an addictive gambling pattern.

Let Me Buy

Some men who always pay for the food, entertainment, and comforts of others delight in the feelings of power that come from being the first to get out the wallet and pay. They may spend compulsively in their need to control.

Vicarious Pleasure

Some men spend very little themselves but seem to take great pleasure in giving money to others and watching them spend. These spenders cannot say no to spouses, friends, and children when they want money, but they resist buying for themselves. They may become fixed on supplying cash and credit to others. In these circumstances, spending is a vicarious experience.

Men often cannot return merchandise they have bought compulsively, and they beg and bribe others to return it for them. Relieved of the burden, they experience great relief. Men who are compulsive spenders also tend to be reluctant to give away or discard clothes, tools, and other purchased items.

The behavioral patterns described in this chapter are not neat and immutable. They may overlap—a person may display more than one spending style. Although our culture disparages and stereotypes women as shoppers, money addiction is not limited to one gender, but afflicts both men and women.

5

Phases of Compulsive Spending

Like other addictions, compulsions about money do not usually develop suddenly. Instead they progress through phases. Characteristics of each phase are hallmarks so typical and identifiable that they indicate the progressive seriousness of the condition.

Phase One: Warning

A person in phase one of compulsive spending engages in the behavior primarily for emotional relief. The problem may progress to loss of control but does not invariably do so. The warning phase is the best time for changes in patterns. The earlier compulsive spenders face and accept their addictive behavior, the better their chances for long-term recovery.

Characteristics

- Relief and mood elevation
- Entitlement spending
- Power spending
- Overspending patterns
- Nervousness and irritability
- Increased financial worries
- Guilt and defensiveness

- Confusion

- Spending plans and new resolutions

Relief and Mood Elevation

A lift in mood that results from spending is only a false and temporary fix; long-term feelings of well-being require the resolution of one's deeper problems. Spending may provide appropriate pleasure. A healthy activity becomes a problem when the balance shifts from spending for reward, recreation, and relaxation to spending for relief and mood change. When money is used to numb moods and get emotional distance from real life problems, the balance that keeps things on an even keel has shifted. Spending comes to be seen as the source of good feelings and emotional relief.

Entitlement Spending

Feelings of entitlement ("Life, or the world, owes me") usually come from emotional deprivation and loss. Often it is difficult for people to say no to themselves when they feel empty and unfulfilled. Usually what they really need is love and validation instead of material things. The stronger the sense of entitlement, the easier it is to justify spending in an effort to fill empty emotional places.

Entitlement spending is an unhealthy response to feelings of lonely self-righteousness. People who spend because they "deserve" things may sincerely believe that they should meet their own needs at any cost. Feeling that the world owes them, it is difficult to say no to their perceived needs. Why should they deprive themselves of the expensive tool or silk blouse that they want so badly? Entitlement spenders take deprivation of the things they yearn for as punishment. They may be outraged because they deserved to have their early childhood needs met and did not. Entitlement spending is usually very emotional. They subconsciously fill their lives with material goods to make up for lost emotional nurturing. Enough is never enough, no matter how many material possessions they have.

Power Spending

When people who lack sufficient personal power and self-esteem begin to equate power with money, it may become their god. Their spending is an ego extension, an effort to show others that the spender has value and is in control. Their relationship to money is marked by a pattern of extravagance and grandiosity. These people buy the best and the most in an attempt to control internal insecurities and low self-esteem. Being demanding with sales clerks and making last-minute grandiose statements ("Oh, and throw in the gold bracelet, too") are common symptoms of power spending.

Overspending Patterns

The warning phase is the period when individual overspending patterns initially develop. It doesn't matter whether people are binge spenders, TV shoppers, or money jugglers—all may develop a fairly regular pattern of overspending behavior.

Overspending kept Ted and Katie locked in a financial prison of their own making. They had spent everything in their checking account, their paychecks weren't due for two more weeks, and the bills hadn't been paid. To top off their trouble, the rent was overdue, so they wiped out their savings account to bail themselves out. Then the same crisis happened again. This time they didn't have any savings to use, so they begged a large loan from Katie's mother. Then they spent themselves into another bind, worse yet because they had increased debt and decreased assets. Eventually they sold one of their cars to make it through the month. Because the pattern slowly developed over the course of two years, Ted and Katie didn't recognize it until they had repeated it so many times they no longer could deny it.

Nervousness and Irritability

As overspending begins to pose an ever increasing array of problems, people become nervous and irritable. They are short-tempered or walk around quietly brooding. They often are irritated with themselves and others. Something deep down inside of them suggests that their actions are the problem, not someone or something else, and that is irritating. They may take things said innocently by others as personal criticism; they feel nervous, anxious, and very uncomfortable.

In this phase, their emotional distress can work for or against them. It can be interpreted as a signal to change their use of money and stop the progression of compulsive spending in its tracks, or it can serve as the impetus for more spending.

Increased Financial Worries

Overspending hits home when the bills arrive. Overspenders may be so out of touch with the reality of their overspending that they cannot see that more spending means more bills to pay. Overdue notes and letters from collection agencies, landlords, mortgage companies, and other creditors increase their financial worries.

Of course, the more threatening the messages are, the more worried people become. The worry, if they allow it to grow, can turn into panic and paranoia, the feeling that everyone is out to get them. Recognized early, the worry can alert them to their problem spending, allowing them to make some changes before it controls them.

Guilt and Defensiveness

Compulsive spenders feel guilty when they use their compulsive behavior to avoid problems. Nevertheless, the more they count on the high, the less they want to give it up. Defensiveness results when people attempt to bury their guilt in order to continue spending. They deny the problem when anyone or anything reminds them of the lurking feelings of guilt they are trying to quash.

Confusion

The more compulsive spending becomes, the more confused the spenders feel emotionally. When spending begins to be used as a sedative to avoid real life problems, it generates a discontented feeling, a sense of confusion and lack of direction. Thinking patterns lose clarity when spenders are involved in their compulsive behavior, and they may feel that they're walking slightly off their emotional balance beams. Unable to focus consistently on the cause and solution of their problem, they seem to jump from thought to thought and wander in circles as they make half-hearted attempts to clarify and direct their lives. At times the discomfort caused by their confusion and mounting anxiety does give them an extra push to get things running smoothly again by confronting their spending.

Spending Plans and New Resolutions

The recognition of an emerging pattern causes overspenders to make resolutions about changing their spending behavior. Healthy spenders at this point can make plans and stick to them. Compulsive spenders may be able to plan, but the difference is that they are unable to follow through reliably. Instead they sabotage their own resolutions and continue in the cycle of compulsive spending. Unlike healthy spenders, who discern that their behavior is getting out of hand, money abusers begin the descent into the second phase.

Phase Two: Loss of Control

Major life disruptions begin to occur as compulsive spending patterns and rituals increase and escalate. Crossing over the line from *choosing to spend* and feeling that you *must spend* marks the change.

Characteristics
- Preoccupation and obsession
- Spending more to feel the same effect
- Secrets and lying
- Mood swings
- Rationalizations
- Euphoric recall
- Broken promises
- Increasing disorder
- Maintenance spending
- Frantic thinking
- Memory loss
- Escape attempts

Preoccupation and Obsession

The more people run away from life into spending, the more removed and distracted they become from their real problems. Hiding from problems in spending becomes a full-time job. Planning, scheming, and spending rituals develop into preoccupations that devour a major part of the day. A primary obsession develops that focuses on perpetuating the spending cycle.

Having crossed the line from choice to compulsion, people in the second phase heighten their spending fervor and seem to acquire new energy. Buying five newspapers and reading sale ads to find the "perfect bargain," they may not notice dirty dishes, smelly laundry, and uncut grass. Spending plans, schemes, and worries may disrupt their sleep. Work may be interrupted by extended lunch periods, excessive personal calls, and general degeneration of performance, productivity, and attendance.

Relationships often are strained to the breaking point and sometimes beyond while friends and relatives struggle to figure out what has happened to their lives. Health problems may develop as stress and emotional discontent increase. Illness may become a way to hide, subconsciously or not, and avoid facing the world. Spiritual values and habits decay; legal problems may mount. The obsession may impair all facets of a person's life: personal needs, relationships, employment, and leisure.

Spending More to Feel the Same Effect

The compulsive spending cycle does not have healthy limits. A few hours of shopping used to take the edge off the spender's stress, but now the spender needs to shop longer and buy more to get that good, relaxed feeling. Thinking becomes distorted during a spending binge. If buying a basketball used to make a person feel good, now he needs to buy a ball, a net, and new basketball shoes. With the avalanche of problems and loss of self-esteem comes the increased need to dull the pain of living. People caught in out-of-control spending may plunge deeper into the compulsion. What used to be the "spending break" has become the short-term "spending fix."

Secrets and Lying

Lying and secrets develop when others challenge, interrupt, or question the behavior. A compulsive spender comes to rely on the initially soothing use of money as if it were a primary and essential life source. When the behavior is threatened the automatic response is to cover up the seriousness of the problem.

The woman who used to hide new clothes only in the trunk of her car now stashes them in other secret hiding places and declares that a new outfit is old. A man pads his bowling expenses to cover the cost of yet another workbench gadget. A fabricated business lunch explains money used for another pair of shoes. After a while, it is hard to remember what one told whom, and lies cover up other lies.

Mood Swings

As compulsive behavior progresses, a person begins to live "two lives." The secret life needs to be protected at all costs. Walking a tightrope causes mood swings and changes. Neither the spender nor family and friends know what to expect. Life becomes a nightmare. Loved ones feel especially vulnerable because spenders' defenses cause them to blame others for problems.

Compulsive spenders control others by means of their moods. People start to "walk on eggs" around them, which suits them perfectly. Spenders do not want to be confronted; their mood swings assure that no one will dare.

Rationalizations

Sometimes compulsive spenders are aware that their rationalizations falsely explain their behavior. "I've got to come up with some credible reason for buying the new sofa" a person might tell himself. "There must be some way to justify charging it." Sometimes, however, they rationalize on a subconscious level: "I have every right to buy new wallpaper, even if I can't afford it, because I've been under so much stress lately. It relaxes me to do projects around the apartment. I may overspend at times, but at least I'm not an alcoholic like so-and-so."

After a while, people can rationalize just about anything. This defense against knowledge of the truth becomes a honed skill that replaces all logic with plausible but false explanations for unjustifiable actions.

Euphoric Recall

The experience of this delusion is like remembering the lovely steak dinner on a flight from Chicago to Los Angeles and blocking out the fact that the plane crashed after the meal. Denise finds herself in the grip of euphoric recall when she has an urge to go shopping. She feels compelled to jump in the car and head straight downtown. She anticipates the excitement of making even one purchase. What she doesn't remember is how it felt when MasterCard told her to cut up her card and send it back. She doesn't remember the remorse that often follows one of her shopping trips. Nor does she remember the last time she overspent and felt so low that she seriously questioned the value of her existence.

When such haunting memories intrude on compulsive spenders' euphoria, they push them aside. I don't want to think about my debts now, they tell themselves; now I want to concentrate on which credit card I can use to charge that watch. Often, however, their subconscious shields them from the truth. The good feelings and memories return to the forefront of their thoughts, dampening the motivations for change.

Broken Promises

As compulsive spenders walk deeper into their obsession, they lose their ability to honor commitments and keep promises, like any other addict. Jim promised his wife he would take the family to the zoo but instead dragged his disappointed and reluctant family around a flea market all day. Nanette broke her promise to meet friends for lunch in order to go shopping. Margaret promised her children she would take them to the park but wound up pushing the stroller from store to store at the mall. Ken promised his partner he wouldn't charge any more personal expenses to the business but did so anyway. It's not that these people are dishonorable; the compulsion is so powerful that it makes their choices for them.

Increasing Disorder

Inability to predict spending behavior consistently is evidence of powerlessness and loss of control. When loss of control occurs, a person is deeply caught in the spending cycle of good resolutions, broken promises, spending imbalances, remorse, and then a return to good resolutions. Loss of control is progressive. *Having* to spend instead of *choosing* to spend is the terrifying characteristic that denotes a loss of control.

The longer people are caught in the cycle of obsessive compulsive spending, the greater the loss of control. No matter how many times they promise themselves or others they won't overspend, they find that they have lost the ability to spend consistently according to their own intentions. Disruptions in major areas of life become evident as spending takes on a life of its own.

Maintenance Spending

Spending cannot sustain good feelings when it is out of control and causing major life disruptions. Spending more to recapture the high doesn't work; in fact, it causes more pain than joy.

What used to be great fun now leaves the spender feeling guilty and depressed. Shopping no longer acts as a "fix" but has become a joyless obsession. Nevertheless, the addiction compels further repetition of the problem behavior to soothe emotions and to avoid the withdrawal that results from reality.

Even though spending no longer produces a high, at least it staves off the low that accompanies the cessation of compulsive behavior. The symptoms include intense fear, agitation, depression, and panic as well as physical manifestations like sleep problems, dizziness, perspiration, headaches, upset stomach, and heart palpitations.

Frantic Thinking

Compulsive, obsessive activity obscures orderly thought. Problem solving abilities become muddled. Energy pours into obsessive worrying instead of problem solving. Thoughts jump distractedly from one topic to another, and the disorganization hinders clear assessment and planning.

"If I shop at the boutique, I can look for some blue slacks to match the new sweater," a woman might think, "but I need some lipstick, too. I can explain the new things by saying Sophie gave them to me for my birthday. I wonder if there are any messages on the answering machine. There might be a good sale at Duggins's, and I'm worried about Mom's eyes, and we should make plans for the Fourth of July, and the new sweater might be better with a print. . . ." Agitated thought becomes characteristic.

Memory Loss

The deeper compulsive spenders get into the obsessive cycle of spending binges, the harder it is for them to remember what happened. Time seems to fade into the background as the spending cycle takes over. The behavior at this point is often automatic and reactive instead of planned and thought out. The compulsive spender's brain seems to shut down during the cycle. The later effort to remember the specific purchases is painful. Sometimes people cannot remember a shopping trip without looking at the new goods for clues.

These periods of amnesia can be very frightening as a spender tries to put together the forgotten fragmented pieces of a day by using crumpled cash register receipts or asking veiled questions.

Escape Attempts

Feeling desperate and out of control, the compulsive spender tries to escape or change the environment. These efforts are seen as possible, hopeful solutions to the problem. A new relationship, job, house, or city may be considered hopefully as a cure for a person's loss of control. True, a new setting, situation, or person may bring temporary relief; unless the real issues are addressed and resolved, however, efforts to evade the issues fail. Escape attempts generally add to the problems already present in the life of the overspender.

Phase Three: Deterioration Phase

The final phase in the downward spiral of compulsive spending is marked by extreme losses, dread, collapse of self-esteem, isolation, and despair. Often people suffer bouts of severe depression or panic attacks. Uncertain how to reconstruct their lives, addicts in the third phase are headed toward collapse.

Characteristics

- Extreme fear and hopelessness
- Divorce and other relationship breakups
- Bankruptcy and other legal maneuvers
- Collapse of self-esteem
- Collapse of the alibi system
- Chaos
- Ethical erosion
- Isolation and despair

Extreme Fear and Hopelessness

Fears mount, producing continuous panic in the pit of compulsive spenders' stomachs. General feelings of doom and terror become their constant companions. They may wake up at night in a cold sweat, out of breath, and running from a faceless dream monster. Physical complaints and illness increase as their bodies exhibit their emotional pain. So many things seem wrong that people in the crisis stage of the process feel hopeless. They think this disaster must be happening to someone else. How did they ever get so sick and confused?

Paranoia grips them, making them think that someone or something is going to get them at every corner. Their world seems to have lost all of its safe havens when they wake up each morning, terrified to put their feet on the floor.

Divorce and Other Breakups

Compulsive spending and its resulting life disruptions may destroy significant relationships. A healthy level of intimacy is impossible when one or both partners have lost control over their behavior.

Tom's wife Kathy filed for divorce the day a truck pulled up to repossess the new snowmobile Tom had presented to the kids a few months earlier. She said that while she watched the truck pull away, it occurred to her that if she didn't divorce Tom, she would lose bits of herself until nothing was left.

Sandy left her husband, although she was the compulsive spender.

They had an unspoken agreement that he wouldn't bother her about her spending and she wouldn't mention his affairs. He broke the silent code. That was enough to send Sandy to divorce court rather than change her spending patterns.

Bankruptcy and Other Legal Maneuvers

Compulsive spenders in the crisis stage declare bankruptcy and try other legal maneuvers. They see these ploys as solutions to their problems, believing that they will be perfectly able to put their financial lives back in order. Reality almost never matches that fantasy. Financial schemes don't remedy the compulsion, which remains unaltered.

Collapse of Self-Esteem

Shamed by behaviors out of their control, spenders begin to detest themselves and their own feelings of helplessness. Not understanding the power of the cycle they have become involved in, they begin to believe that in fact they are worthless and helpless to change.

They even may begin to hate their own image and avoid looking in mirrors. They neglect routine grooming, putting off haircuts and even daily bathing. Often they feel like walking shells of their old selves trapped in bodies that they have little energy or love for. They feel ashamed of their lives and believe that not only have they made mistakes but they are *themselves* mistakes. Deep depressions, escape into other addictions, and apathy may accompany the collapse of self-esteem. Thoughts of suicide may occur and even plans to carry out the thoughts.

Collapse of the Alibi System

Rationalization and denial eventually wear out. Spenders may get momentary glimpses of truth. Stripped of their defenses, they see the destructiveness of their spending patterns. Nothing they say can reasonably explain their irrational behavior. They have run out of excuses, explanations, fabrications, and lies.

Chaos

Unable to deny their problem, compulsive spenders will then face chaos in many areas of their lives. In this end phase of compulsive spending, usually the pervasive damage brings about a major crisis that challenges the spender to confront the sweeping effects of the compulsion.

Connie believed that everything that possibly could go wrong had done so. She was wrong. One evening, while she was hosting a dinner party for her boss and his wife, a "repo" man arrived at her doorstep, asking for the keys to her car. Connie's position at work? A loan officer! The chaos spreads in proportion to the growing compulsion.

Ethical Erosion

Hopelessness often produces a lack of concern for traditional values, sometimes prompting spenders to illegal behavior. Because they feel trapped, helpless, and alone, they may break the law in a futile, last-ditch attempt to save themselves. They may forget their treasured values, acting out in ways that previously would have appalled them. They feel backed up against a wall, completely unable to see how they are caught in the claws of a progressive, obsessive-compulsive disorder. Shoplifting, fraud, extortion, blackmail, prostitution and other illegal activities that once would have shocked them are seen now as the only way out.

Isolation and Despair

Faced with the true reality of their problem, compulsive spenders attempt to withdraw from other people. They don't like themselves or anyone else. Suicidal thinking and planning intensify unless they choose to use their remaining energy to seek help.

Jamie hid in the bedroom of his apartment for three days, so despondent over his financial situation that he wished to see no one. When his sister discovered him, he had just finished writing his suicide note.

6

Inventory for Spending Phases

The following workbook section is intended to help you more specifically identify and acknowledge your own compulsive spending. The awareness you have developed from reviewing the Compulsive Spending Survey (chapter 3) will assist you in answering the questions. Awareness that you may have a spending problem challenges you to look deeper into its roots and patterns. People gain power as they learn about the connections between their histories and their money abuse. The following inventory is a stepping stone on the road to freedom and honesty about money. Approach this work with a willingness to examine in detail all of your money history, feelings, secrets, and experiences. The greater your willingness to be honest and thorough, the greater will be your progress.

People who have dug into their past and present money behaviors and motives have received the gift of healing insights. The inventory experience is powerful. It quickly moves people who abuse money into the light of a new reality.

Relief and Mood Elevation

How and when have I used my spending to change and control my moods?

_____

_____

_____

_____

What feelings am I trying to relieve or change when I spend?

_____

_____

_____

_____

Entitlement Spending

List specific times when you have felt "entitled" to spend.

_____

_____

_____

_____

_____

How have your feelings of entitlement harmed you?

_____

_____

_____

_____

Power Spending

When and how have you used spending to elevate your ego and make you feel more powerful?

_____

_____

_____

_____

What deeper needs might you be trying to fulfill when you spend? Some needs may be comfort, acceptance, respect, intimacy, and love. Describe how the needs and the spending are related.

_____

_____

_____

_____

Overspending Patterns

Describe your first memories of overspending.

_____

_____

_____

_____

How has your overspending affected the major areas of your life, such as family, work, sex, and friendship?

_____

_____

_____

_____

Nervousness and Irritability

List the ways in which compulsive spending contributes to your nervousness and irritability.

_____

_____

_____

_____

_____

What feelings do you think are covered up by your nervousness and irritability?

_____

_____

_____

_____

Increased Financial Worries

What three things worry you most about your spending and finances?

_____

_____

_____

How does your spending contribute to your financial worries?

_____

_____

_____

_____

_____

Guilt and Defensiveness

Specifically, how does your spending cause you to feel guilty?

_____

_____

_____

_____

_____

In what manner and to whom have you been defensive about your spending behavior?

_____

_____

_____

_____

Confusion

How is your ability to think and reason clearly affected by your spending?

_____

_____

_____

_____

How does your spending behavior contribute to the confusion in your life?

_____

_____

_____

_____

Spending Plans and New Resolutions

Write a brief history of your attempts to control and change your spending behavior with plans, resolutions, and budgets.

_____

_____

_____

_____

_____

_____

List any ways in which you have sabotaged your budgets and spending plans and resolutions.

_____

_____

_____

_____

_____

Phase Two: Loss of Control

Preoccupation and Obsession

Describe a situation in which you were obsessed with spending.

_____

_____

_____

_____

How has your self-esteem been affected by your preoccupation with spending?

_____

_____

_____

_____

_____

Spending More to Feel the Same Effect

When and how has your spending behavior increased and accelerated?

_____

_____

_____

_____

What methods have you used to maintain and temporarily increase your "good spending feelings"?

_____

_____

_____

_____

_____

Secrets and Lying

What are some of the lies you have told others about your spending behavior?

_____

_____

_____

What is your biggest spending secret?

_____

_____

_____

_____

_____

Mood Swings

How do you feel before, during, and after spending?

_____

_____

_____

_____

_____

How do your moods change as a result of spending?

_____

_____

_____

_____

_____

Rationalizations

What untrue explanations have you given for your spending?

_____

_____

_____

_____

How do you attempt to get other people "off your back" about your spending and money issues?

_____

_____

_____

_____

_____

Euphoric Recall

List areas of your spending that still bring you "good memories."

_____

_____

_____

_____

How does remembering the "good money times" keep you distracted from the problems in your life caused by your money abuse?

_____

_____

_____

_____

Broken Promises

When has your spending caused you to break promises to others?

_____

_____

_____

_____

When has your spending caused you to break promises to yourself?

_____

_____

_____

_____

_____

Increasing Disorder

What areas of your spending behavior are out of control?

_____

_____

_____

_____

_____

List examples of times when you were unable to spend according to your intentions.

_____

_____

_____

_____

_____

Maintenance Spending

What are your specific problems with maintenance spending?

_____

_____

_____

_____

_____

List ways in which you play games with money despite your promises not to do so.

_____

_____

_____

_____

_____

Frantic Thinking

Describe your thinking patterns and level of concentration when you have felt the best in your life.

_____

_____

_____

_____

What is your thinking and concentration like before, during, and after a spending episode?

_____

_____

_____

_____

Memory Loss

Write about any memory loss or "blank spots" you have experienced before, during, or after spending.

_____

_____

_____

_____

Write about things you've forgotten to do because you were so focused on spending and all that surrounds it.

_____

_____

_____

_____

Escape Attempts

How have you changed the circumstances of your life in efforts to change your spending behavior?

_____

_____

_____

_____

Why do you think your escape attempts failed?

_____

_____

_____

_____

Phase Three: Deterioration

Extreme Fear and Hopelessness

What are your worst fears about your spending?

_____

_____

_____

_____

Explain how you have lost hope about your situation.

_____

_____

_____

_____

_____

Divorce and Other Relationship Breakups

If you are divorced or separated, how did spending contribute to the breakup?

_____

_____

_____

_____

If you are living with a spouse or partner, how often do you think about ending the relationship? Is your spouse or partner considering it?

_____

_____

_____

_____

Bankruptcy and Other Legal Maneuvers

Have you ever declared bankruptcy? What motivated you to do so?

_____

_____

_____

_____

Are you contemplating bankruptcy now? If so, what are your motives?

_____

_____

_____

_____

Collapse of Self-Esteem

In what ways has your self-esteem increasingly been affected by your spending?

_____

_____

_____

_____

_____

Describe how the effects of your spending behavior have caused you to neglect your personal needs or care of yourself.

_____

_____

_____

_____

_____

Collapse of the Alibi System

Have your explanations and excuses stopped working for you?

_____

_____

_____

_____

_____

How and why have these defenses failed?

_____

_____

_____

_____

_____

Chaos

Describe the major imbalances in your life.

_____

_____

_____

_____

_____

How has your spending contributed to these problems or caused them?

_____

_____

_____

_____

_____

Ethical Erosion

How have you violated your values as a result of your spending behavior?

_____

_____

_____

_____

_____

In what ways do your values and standards differ from those of five years ago?

_____

_____

_____

_____

Isolation and Despair

Describe all of the ways you have "hit bottom" with your spending and money obsessions.

_____

_____

_____

_____

_____

_____

_____

_____

How has your spiritual life been affected by your spending?

_____

_____

_____

_____

_____

_____

Additional Inventory Questions

In what ways do you resist honesty about your spending behavior?

_____

_____

_____

_____

_____

_____

_____

List any specific fears that keep you from getting help and making changes in your life.

_____

_____

_____

_____

_____

_____

_____

_____

Who would be pleased if you changed your spending behavior? Who would be displeased?

_____

_____

_____

_____

_____

What would be the single most difficult thing to change or give up about your spending behavior?

_____

_____

_____

_____

_____

_____

How might shame keep you paralyzed in your problems?

_____

_____

_____

_____

_____

_____

A spending inventory is work in progress. It is something to be done periodically. Each time you take it, you will learn more about yourself. It not only allows you to see more of what is hurting you, it lets you see your personal growth as well. It shows you that you are honest and courageous. The spending inventory gives you the opportunity to see how you are hurting yourself and how you may allow others to hurt you. You have the option to choose healthy attitudes, behaviors, and relationships.

We recommend that readers take the spending inventory now and review it again after reading the rest of the book.

7

Poverty Addiction

People whose lives have become unmanageable because of money generally either overspend or underspend. Poverty addiction is characterized by a downward spiral of deprivation that increasingly limits the persons' lives. They have the means and potential to meet their needs for adequate shelter, food, clothing, health care, and "extras" such as creative outlets and social activities. Despite their ability to buy what they need, however, they systematically deprive themselves.

Poverty addicts may overspend in one area, leaving themselves unable to cover necessities. They may leave well-paid jobs for jobs that pay minimum wage. Then they leave those jobs for none at all. These people cannot bring themselves to dream. They are so adapted to deprivation that they cannot visualize a more abundant life. Their future promises only more severe want as things become smaller, more limited, more bleak. Poverty addicts drop even non material pleasures, such as friends, exercise, diet, and hobbies, because they represent a fullness inconsistent with the small life.

The following story provides a glimpse of how a person can adjust to pain as a companion and then turn that relationship into poverty addiction.

Marty's Story

As a child, Marty had but one dream—to please his father. He tried everything. He worked hard at school and came home with straight As. Marty imagined his father reacting to the good news with praise or even a man-to-man handshake. Instead his father bellowed, "If you could do this good now, why didn't you do this good last time?" When Marty was voted most valuable player by his baseball team, his father met the news with the remark, "Well, it's about time!"

One day someone left cigarettes in the bathroom. Although Marty was innocent, his father blamed him and beat him severely with a leather belt. After the whipping, the true culprit came forward, confessed, and also was beaten. All that Marty's father said to him was, "Well, that's for all the times you got away with something!"

Beatings and verbal put-downs were the father's primary means of communication with his children. Although Marty's mother was at home, her fear of her husband prevented her defending or protecting the children.

Marty spent a lot of time wondering whether he would always be a loser, whether he would ever be strong enough, fast enough, smart enough, or courageous enough to please his father. Marty continuously felt driven to prove his worth, except when he visited his grandparents. They owned a tavern and knew every one of their customers by name. When Marty visited them, he felt like a celebrity. His grandmother let him go into the freezer and help himself to ice-cream bars. His grandfather proudly showed him off to anyone who would listen. The tavern felt safe and secure. There Marty temporarily relaxed and let his guard down.

Unfortunately, some sort of disagreement occurred between Marty's grandparents and his father. He suddenly announced that the kids no longer would be allowed to visit their grandparents or even to speak to them again. The reason was never explained. Marty's only safe place was taken from him with no apology.

When he was old enough to leave home, Marty believed that he had come up with his last and most promising plan for earning his father's respect. He made a family announcement, proudly breaking the news that he had joined the marines, as his father had done many years before.

"What the heck did you do that for?" his father asked.

"Because you always said you hoped one of your sons would be man enough to be a marine," Marty said.

"I'm still hoping," his father said before turning and walking out of the room.

Marty's needs to be heard, nurtured, praised, accepted, and touched in a loving way were never met. His parents' behavior suggests that they had many unmet needs as well. It is difficult for parents to fulfill others' needs, even those of their children, if their own needs have not been served. People can give only what they have. If they are empty inside, they have little or nothing to pass on to others.

When he reached adulthood, Marty's spending behavior reflected these attitudes:

Worthlessness

"I don't deserve anything."

"I'm unlovable."

"I'm incompetent."

Disappointment

"If I don't want anything, at least I won't be disappointed."

"Trying isn't worth the effort."

Martyrdom

"I am a victim."

"People let me down."

Isolation

"I am alone."

"No one understands."

Domination

"The more I control myself and others, the less I will get hurt."

"Other people can be controlled through sarcasm, intimidation, and manipulation."

Marty married immediately after returning home from Vietnam. Throughout the marriage he had many opportunities to make a better living, but he always stayed almost at poverty level, despite his high marks in college. He permitted his wife, Robin, no freedom to spend money, but made even the smallest spending decisions himself. *He* would decide whether Robin *really* needed a new spring blouse or not. If they had company for Easter, Marty planned the menu and budget. If Robin took a job to make some extra money, Marty earned less. If Robin observed that they needed a new car, Marty scoffed, "I guess nothing's good enough for you, is it?"

Robin began to notice that they didn't have many friends. She suspected that people knew they couldn't afford to join them at a restaurant or movie and consequently stopped calling. She was uncomfortably aware that other people seemed to feel sorry for them. At night when she lay still beside Marty, she felt too tired and too sorry for Marty to leave him.

Marty vented some of his anger, using her as the target and belittling her. By earning low wages and not even trying to perform close to his financial potential, Marty could remain in the only role he had ever known: the role of failure. He learned early that effort just sets one up for disappointment. Even though he had a wife who was thrilled to be married to him (he had a good education and was attractive), his self-esteem was so low that he believed, probably subconsciously, that he didn't deserve and couldn't trust himself to keep anything nice like a loving wife or an occasional dinner out or some decent furniture or a vacation now and then.

The Big Payoff

What is the emotional payoff? *Why* would anyone be a poverty addict? Given a choice, wouldn't most people rather be *anything* but a poverty addict?

But people don't get the opportunity to choose their misery. An alcoholic doesn't wake up one day and say, "By George, today I think I'll start drinking alcoholically. Or maybe I could get a good cocaine habit going!" People experiment, usually without realizing that's what they're doing. *Bingo!* Something, some substance or behavior, numbs pain, and so they repeat it. Addicts repeat it despite the fact that eventually it causes more problems.

Poverty addicts experience certain psychological "benefits" from their deprivation, which hurts them but perversely meets some unconscious need. They are not at fault, for they do not voluntarily seek these "payoffs":

- They feel martyred.

- They control other people. They can make them go away (like Robin and Marty's friends) or make them stay (like Robin). They cause such anxiety that others walk on eggs around them, afraid of saying the wrong thing, always skirting issues of money.

- They are takers, taking joy, spontaneity, abundance, and comforts from themselves and loved ones. Yet they may be seen as self-sacrificing, thrifty, righteous, and simple people.

- They have all of the power (Robin can't make a move without Marty's permission).

- They seldom are disappointed or become vulnerable because they never want anything.

- They keep people connected to them through money. Others are forced to plead, beg, tiptoe, reason, and negotiate to deal with them.

- They remain victims who can justify their misery. After all, who *wouldn't* be miserable in their shoes?

Poverty addicts are not misers, grasping people who live wretchedly in order to hoard their wealth. They rarely have any wealth to hoard; if they do, they don't share it with anybody, not even themselves. They systematically prevent wealth and abundance from coming into their lives. If they do have wealth, they declare it off-limits. Of course, people are hurt by the poverty addict's behavior. If Mom denies herself new eyeglasses and dental checkups, chances are she also denies those things to her children.

To illustrate, here is a typical pattern of events that helps teach a *desirable* behavior: a boy tries to be successful in school and receives good grades. His parents praise him and he is the center of their attention. Since he likes the praise and attention, he repeats the behavior that brought it to him. He feels successful and has learned that his efforts pay off. Eventually he comes to expect that he will do well. He trusts himself.

In contrast, Marty was punished for doing well in school. He learned that his efforts were meaningless. He began to think, I must be pretty bad if my father won't accept me and my mother won't protect me. Marty learned that, whenever he set himself up for approval, his father always shot him down. Wishing to protect himself from such pain, he now expects nothing good from life, thus avoiding vulnerability. All of his experience makes Marty mad, but to whom can he express his rage? Himself—and his own wife and children.

Pam's Story

Like Marty, Pam grew up believing that something was wrong with her, that her parents' neglect reflected her inadequacy and unlovable character. In her childhood, she lived in a big house with all the trappings of success. Her father was a workaholic who seldom came home. Mom was always sick in her bedroom with some vague ailment. From the age of five, Pam fended for herself.

Often Pam's needs and desires were dismissed because Mother was too sick and Dad too busy to attend to the child's needs. Her parents gave her elaborate birthday parties but never asked her what gift she might like or what kind of party she would enjoy. Her mother bought her clothes without consulting Pam about styles or colors. Her father bought a piano for her but never asked whether she wanted to play the instrument. Today Pam describes a childhood abundant in things but impoverished nevertheless.

During high school, her friends, guests at her birthday parties, told her what great parents she had. Pam began to think that perhaps her friends were right. Maybe she was crazy. Her mother said she loved her, but somehow Pam didn't feel loved. Eventually she convinced herself that something was wrong with her. She hoarded her money from an after-school job. Unlike the other girls, she denied herself outings and movies, clothes and make-up—all of the things her friends were interested in.

After a while, she denied herself friends as well. She began to think of them as too materialistic and foolhardy. Although Pam went to college and graduated with honors, she was unable to hold a job for long. Her apartment was scantily furnished. She never bought anything personal like clothes or perfume, believing that, if you had *some* clothes, you didn't need more. And if you didn't absolutely *need* something, you shouldn't buy it. When she worked, Pam earned a nice salary, but she always found an excuse to quit jobs shortly after she was hired.

One year her winter boots had holes worn through both soles. Although she had some money in her checking account, instead of taking them to a shoe repair shop or buying new ones, she covered pieces of cardboard with plastic wrap and inserted them in the boots over the holes. Of course the strategy didn't work, and her feet were chronically cold and wet all winter long. If I have boots, she told herself, I don't need another pair.

Pam had developed a life pattern of fixing and patching, never replacing. Practically everything she owned was held together by some homemade repair job. All the while she had the means to earn an income that would have allowed her to replace her badly worn necessities.

One morning, while she was shaking some cinnamon into her coffee grounds, Pam decided the cinnamon habit had to stop. This is an indulgence I can't afford, she thought. Soon everything in her life was bone bare. Her friends were few, jobs were short-lived, she permitted herself no vacations, no new clothes, no extras like cinnamon or nail polish. Pam lived an existence of deprivation and scarcity. Although she cared deeply for a man, a warm, loving relationship just didn't fit into the life of a poverty addict.

John gave Pam an expensive and very beautiful ring as a symbol of his love for her. He previously had given her smaller gifts, which she accepted with embarrassment and then put away, never to open them again. The ring was in a different category, unacceptable to her.

This is too much, she thought. I could never wear it without feeling embarrassed. As these thoughts raced through her head, Pam knew there was no chance she could *ever* accept a gift so expensive and meaningful. She told John she didn't like it—plain and simple, easy as that. John had known Pam long enough to realize she was lying. Before storming out of the door, ring in hand, he shouted, "You're just like Groucho Marx. You wouldn't want to be a member of a club that would have you as a member!"

John's parting remark hit home. Pam knew he was absolutely right. Shortly after that Pam went to her first Debtors Anonymous meeting. There she met people just like herself. For the first time in her life, she began to believe that she was important.

Poverty Addiction Survey

The first step in recovery from illness is an accurate diagnosis. If you don't know what is the matter, you can't fix it. If poverty addiction has you by the neck, you can't shake it loose until you know it's there. Below, phrased as questions, are sixteen common feelings and behaviors of people who are poverty addicts. By honestly answering these questions you can determine how closely your feelings and behaviors resemble those of poverty addicts.

1. Do people similar to you in education and experience tend to make a lot more money than you? ☐ Yes ☐ No
2. Do you change jobs frequently, always blaming your employer? ☐ Yes ☐ No
3. Are your family members afraid to talk about money with you? ☐ Yes ☐ No
4. Have you gone more than two years without taking a week or more vacation? ☐ Yes ☐ No
5. Do you skip regular dental and eye exams or needed doctor visits because of money? ☐ Yes ☐ No
6. Do friends and family urge you to buy new clothes? ☐ Yes ☐ No

7. Have you ever worried that you might just be extremely lazy? (Poverty addicts are not lazy people, but they sometimes think they are because they can't find another explanation for their behavior.)☐ Yes   ☐ No

8. Do you constantly deprive yourself of necessities?

Groceries	☐ Yes	☐ No
Shoes	☐ Yes	☐ No
Books	☐ Yes	☐ No
School	☐ Yes	☐ No
Medical care	☐ Yes	☐ No
Rent	☐ Yes	☐ No
Heat	☐ Yes	☐ No

9. Do you fear negative consequences if you buy something new for yourself?   ☐ Yes ☐ No

10. What reasons do you have for not buying things for yourself?
"I will not like it." ☐ Yes   ☐ No
"I will regret it."   ☐ Yes   ☐ No
"People will think I'm a spendthrift."   ☐ Yes ☐ No
"I feel guilty afterward."   ☐ Yes   ☐ No
"I will be ashamed of my purchases."   ☐ Yes ☐ No
"Others will not approve." ☐ Yes   ☐ No

11. Do you feel cheated because you live so minimally?
☐ Yes   ☐ No

12. Do you overspend in one area? For example, do you buy more groceries than you can consume?   ☐ Yes ☐ No

13. Do you feel that others are selfish and self-centered when they express a desire to buy something? ☐ Yes   ☐ No

14. Do you become angry when families or friends buy you something nice?   ☐ Yes ☐ No

15. Do you have a cache of unopened gifts?   ☐ Yes ☐ No

16. Do you often feel anxious about money?   ☐ Yes ☐ No

These questions are not to test you but to help you assess your deprivation. If you answered yes to several questions, you may need help to examine further the causes of your self-denial and its painful effects in your life.

Recovery from Poverty Addiction

If the poverty addict gets some sort of emotional payoff for staying addicted to poverty, what would he receive if he traded that life in for abundance? Those who have made that choice and are now in a recovery program say that the biggest reward is feeling valuable. They want to protect and nurture themselves. If they care for themselves well, then they're strong and secure enough to be generous with others. If they love themselves, they feel worthy of intimate relationships, material necessities and the extras, the abundance that gives flavor and richness to life.

The addiction to scarcity is just as powerful as any other addiction, and it brings as much pain. If pain becomes familiar and tolerable enough, poverty addicts stick with it, embracing its familiarity. They settle for the distorted comforts of recognizable, customary pain.

Where to Look for Help

The fellowship of Debtors Anonymous welcomes poverty addicts. DA is the most effective support group for anyone who abuses money, whether overspending or underspending. Call or write

Debtors Anonymous
General Service Board
P.O. Box 20322
New York, New York 10025-9992
(212) 969-0710

Or call information and ask for the telephone number of Debtors Anonymous in your area.

Many poverty addicts have found recovery and happiness through the fellowship of DA. There are no fees or dues, and only first names are used. The program is based on the Twelve Steps and Twelve Traditions of Alcoholics Anonymous, which support members while allowing them to decide for themselves how fast and how far they want to go.

Counseling and therapy are other important and sometimes necessary adjuncts to DA meetings. A therapist who is knowledgeable about poverty addiction can be an important part of the recovery plan. Chapter 14, "Creating a Recovery Journal," applies to underspenders just as it does to over-spenders. Use the guidelines outlined in that chapter to proceed in your personal recovery.

If you think you may be a poverty addict and are sick and tired of being sick and tired, make an agreement with yourself. Commit yourself to attend DA meetings with an open mind. The support of others who have been in your predicament may give you a slice of the dream, a vision of the full life that has been possible for you all along.

Part Two

The Empty Heart

Ginny's Story Continues

After a while Ginny's juggling of credit card bills, cash advances on one to pay another, requests for increased credit limits, and acquisition of new cards didn't work anymore. Late notices arrived daily and telephone calls continually unnerved her.

One such call from a creditor stood out in her mind as the most humiliating of all. A neighbor, Cathy, and her children were eating lunch in Ginny's kitchen and enjoying a lively conversation. When the phone rang, Ginny reached for it, not missing a beat in her talk with Cathy. The caller was grave and threatening, a creditor who demanded immediate payment and return of Ginny's cut-up credit card. Cathy and the four children sat just a few feet away, in perfect earshot of Ginny's inquisition.

Ginny tried to appease the creditor and fool Cathy at the same time, an act that required a prodigious impromptu performance. Every statement had to be devised in a moment to sound like one thing to Ginny's friend and another to the creditor. As she spoke she felt her face burning with embarrassment. Perspiration trickled down her ribs. She carefully chose her words to suggest that the caller was an employee of her husband, Noel, asking her to intervene on his behalf with her husband. Answers like "You'll have to talk to my husband about that" were devices to buy time with the creditor and save face with Cathy. Finally the caller became exasperated with Ginny's non cooperation and hung up. She said in her most pleasant voice, "Good luck, and thanks for calling. I'll talk to Noel when he comes home."

She casually explained to Cathy that Noel's construction company hired day workers for cash. The caller was one of those men, she said, asking her to persuade Noel to hire him permanently and offer him benefits. Although the story was plausible and fit the dialogue, Ginny knew that her face told a different story. Eventually she stopped inviting people to her home for fear of a repeat performance. Her life narrowed, progressively more isolated and limited as her problem became more serious. Even spending failed her. More and more spending was required to bring the same "high," and eventually no amount of spending was enough. Still, Ginny continued to spend compulsively, trying to numb the feelings of shame, fear, guilt, and worthlessness that plagued her.

Ginny's Childhood

When Ginny was seven, her father died. Her mother told her, "Be brave and don't cry." Ginny was not hugged or consoled but told instead to dress and groom herself well for the relatives who would stop by to offer their condolences. Ginny's feelings were not accepted. Eventually she didn't credit them with any importance either.

Her mother married a second husband, who always made Ginny feel inadequate. On one occasion, she overheard him bragging about her accomplishments. The only problem was that they were all untrue. In Ginny's mind, her stepfather didn't think she was good enough as she was, so he prettied her up to make her more acceptable.

Ginny received almost no physical attention. She interpreted this withholding of affection as an indication that she was unlovable. Other mothers and fathers hugged and kissed and cuddled their children. Ginny took the blame for her mother's coldness.

Ginny felt like an unwelcome intruder in a home where her mother and stepfather seemed very involved in one another. As she grew, her feeling of being an outsider pervaded every aspect of her life, not just her life at home. She thought of the other kids at school as normal, a part of a whole. She regarded herself as a misfit, not belonging to any inner circle. She began to cherish any small compliments or words of acceptance she was offered, even those that had strings attached and were unhealthy. When she was sixteen, for example, a popular boy asked her for a date. He told her to meet him at the school parking lot on Sunday afternoon at one o'clock. Everyone would meet at the school and then go to the zoo for a picnic lunch. Ginny spent hours styling her hair, changing outfits, trying different combinations of makeup, until finally she was pleased with her appearance. She arrived at the school early and waited. She was still there when the sun set. Humiliated about being stood up and dreading the questions of curious parents, she waited until evening to walk home.

The boy never called or apologized. A few months later, he called again and asked her out again. She asked about the broken date. "Oh, that. That was just a big mix-up," he said. "You're not one of those stuck-up girls who hold a grudge, are you?" Ginny said no and accepted the invitation.

It was the first of many relationships with men who always disappointed her. The men treated her as if she didn't count. Since that manner was familiar, Ginny felt quite at home with such men.

Family of Origin

Clearly Ginny's girlhood needs for affirmation, respect, love, and trust were not met. It is very important for people in recovery to think about the needs they had as children. They must see what needs were unmet, for chances are, they remain unmet. As adults, however, people can seek abundance for the child who still lives within them—an abundance of affirmation, consolation, praise, love, acceptance, tolerance, and all other good things. This abundance can begin to warm them now.

An old Chinese proverb says that nobody's family can hang out the sign NOTHING IS THE MATTER HERE. Many people remember a family that seemed perfect when they were young. Ordinarily time reveals the flaws. All families have unique problems, because all are human and, being so, imperfect. People who remember their childhoods as idyllic and gloss over significant pain deny themselves the opportunity to stop perpetuating hurt. This loss is particularly poignant in the story of a woman called Melissa. As a child she felt insignificant and unimportant, for children in her family were treated as though they were worthless. She vividly remembers being injured at play and coming indoors for comfort and protection. Her mother hollered at her for dripping blood on the newly washed floor.

Melissa's needs were never met. As an adult, she continued to feel worthless and vulnerable. She began to value fancy clothes, jewelry, and homes because she thought others noticed her and wanted her company if she appeared wealthy. Sales clerks pampered her, and people complimented her belongings. The attention helped Melissa feel like somebody. Asked about her childhood, Melissa remembered it as having been perfectly normal and healthy. By not remembering it as it was, she missed the opportunity to assess and grieve her unmet needs.

Melissa became so obsessed with spending and juggling to pay bills and "borrowing from Peter to pay Paul" that she didn't have much time for her own children. One day her six year old daughter, with tears streaming down her cheeks, implored her, "Mommy, please don't buy anything!" Melissa confronted something she had not seen before: the realization that she was treating her own children the way she had been treated as a child. She began to recognize the emotional abuse she formerly had been unable to see. Suppressed anger and pain surfaced about her parents' inability to give her any loving physical contact like hugs and cuddling. She felt angry that her parents often had shut her out by speaking a foreign language so she couldn't understand, excluding her from family conversations. And she was angry about never having been complimented or praised or assured of love.

Finding Ways to Use Anger

Of all emotions, many people fear their anger the most. Especially if they were raised in a dysfunctional family—one in which the safe expression of feelings was not modeled or encouraged—they probably are terrified of anger. Many money addicts associate anger with violence, abandonment, verbal abuse, rejection, or the silent treatment, for those were the consequences of anger in their childhood. Additionally, they may fear anger because it has lived within them for so long, brewing just below the surface. They fear they may lose control if they don't keep a tight lid on it. Money addicts who are unable to express anger directly often discharge it in passive-aggressive ways through destructive money behaviors.

People who struggle to express anger are afraid of what they might say and do. They don't trust themselves to control their emotion. They fear they will crumble, fall apart, or become physically violent. Since the safe and healthy expression of anger was not modeled for them, they generally don't have a clue about how to deal with it. If people who suppress emotion don't find safe ways to use it, the force and power of their anger turn inward in self-punishment.

The following strategy may help loosen the grip of anger.

Acknowledge It

Facing one's anger takes patience and courage in an ongoing process. People often need the help and support of other recovering people or a therapist to acknowledge the anger's mere existence, then its intensity. The process can be very painful. Whether they have money issues or not, many people believe that nice men and women don't get angry. They cannot accept the fact that anger is a normal emotion felt by everybody, nice or not.

Anger toward parents sometimes feels particularly "naughty." Melissa initially resisted considering her anger because she felt she was blaming her aged and helpless parents. "What good will it do for me to see the anger I feel toward them?" Melissa asked early in her recovery. "They're too old to change." Her therapist explained that people acknowledge emotions not to change other people but to understand and free themselves. In doing so, they attach some value and importance to their real selves. The expression of anger says, My feelings count; what I feel is important enough to acknowledge.

Express It

Once people decide to "own" their anger by acknowledging its existence, they can begin to express it. Many people benefit from writing their anger in a letter to those who wronged them, deciding later whether to mail it. Other creative endeavors, such as painting or writing a journal, vent the feelings. Talking about the anger when it arises is preferable to letting it build.

If people feel safe, they may decide to express their anger face to face with the person toward whom they feel it. They need to discuss it beforehand with a therapist or someone from DA. They must enter the confrontation knowing that they have no power to change others, desiring to change only themselves. They can control their own reactions but not another's. Talking afterward with people who support them helps them process what happened.

Expressing anger in healthy ways boosts self-esteem. It enables people to feel, some for the first time, that they count.

Let It Go

Unfortunately, it is common for people to skip acknowledging and expressing anger by moving directly to this step and letting it go. Believing it the noble thing to do, they announce to themselves and others that they have let go of their anger. But it usually doesn't go anywhere; it just festers, waiting to be reckoned with. If people have recognized anger and expressed it, however, they may be ready to move toward letting it go and begin grieving the buried hurts. Letting go means that they no longer allow that anger to affect their lives, decisions, and self-image.

Melissa wrote a letter to each parent. The letters did not blame or attack. They simply stated Melissa's feelings and explained their origins. When she put the letters in the mail box, the act symbolized her letting go. Closing the lid on the letters, she declared her release of the anger that once had controlled her. Her action doesn't mean that angry feelings won't resurface. They may. Each of the first three steps measures an ongoing process people incorporate into their lives. When people deal with their anger, they render it powerless to control them.

Forgive Others

Unresolved childhood issues and the resultant feelings of anger, disappointment, and even rage can undermine all that adults strive for. They need to confront the past and then to move on. Forgiveness is the willingness to give up all claims for revenge. Ownership of one's own feelings removes the controlling energy from other persons and returns it to its rightful owner, who may use it creatively to enhance life.

Forgiving is not the same as forgetting. Although Melissa forgave her parents, she keeps her memories. People may wish to forget painful experiences, but that oblivion may not be desirable or helpful. Their past belongs to them. It is their unique history. It says they came from somewhere; they have existed. Like the expression of anger, one forgives for one's own sake. Forgiveness is not a favor to the other but a gift the forgiver offers herself. Without it, an injured person may be unable to relax and enjoy life because doing so would hinder brooding over past hurts. Resentment to spite the "enemy" backfires, however. The object of the anger ironically goes merrily along with life while the angry person remains stuck in the self-pity. Of course, that leads to more compulsive "cover-up-the-real-pain" behavior like overspending, borrowing, and restrictive spending. In other words, the unwillingness to forgive enables the past to continue its damage.

Take a new stance instead: I'm tired of his controlling my thoughts and actions. I'm tired of holding the grudge. I completely forgive in order to get on with my own life. This release doesn't imply condonement of the other's behavior; it simply surrenders the claim for revenge. It pardons the other. When Melissa forgave her parents, she didn't say they were right, and she didn't say they weren't hurtful. She said only that she was making peace with her past so that it no longer could control her. She implied that she was too valuable to allow old hurts to haunt her life.

Forgive Oneself

Sometimes mistakes are terrible, and sometimes the results are terrible. But mistakes are inevitable. They are human. They are even desirable, a privilege; if people never made any mistakes, how would they learn about consequences and the challenge of positive change? One who is a compulsive spender must know that she has made some mistakes. But some people get stuck, seeing their mistakes as indications that they themselves are bad. They fail to separate the error from the person.

Forgiveness of oneself and of others are equally important. Sometimes self-esteem is so low that a person feels unworthy of forgiveness. People "know" this inadequacy for sure, just as they've always known everything for sure. That all-knowing frame of mind might have gotten them into serious trouble. So long as they depreciate themselves, they persist in self-destruction. Perhaps it's time to try another way. If they treat themselves as worthwhile and capable, they begin to feel worthwhile and capable. There's a slogan in the Twelve Step groups (DA, Alcoholics Anonymous, Adult Children of Alcoholics, and others): "Act As If." It means that, if people get the body and the head going in the right direction, the mind and heart will follow.

Melissa found it easier to forgive her parents than herself. She believed she deserved punishment. She did not see that her spending was as severe a penalty as one could find. In her head, she knew she needed to offer herself forgiveness and mercy. But in her heart, she still could not believe it so. Melissa "acted as if." She verbally forgave herself and wrote her forgiveness on paper. She practiced acting as if she loved herself. Eventually she began to feel the part. She ultimately was able to incorporate self-forgiveness into her life.

9

Money Issues for Relationships

Our status-conscious society emphasizes appearances and the accumulation of material goods. It is not surprising that money issues are affecting even the strongest marriages and love relationships. If a relationship already has been weakened by other stresses, money problems can be the fatal blow to the already teetering structure. Even if the relationship is a strong one, money issues can, if not resolved, undermine the commitment between two people, causing serious problems later on.

How Can Something That Started Out So Good Become So Painful?

Healthy relationships are built on a foundation of respect in which the feeling of intimate safety develops. Partners can express themselves freely without fear of attack and feel that their deepest fears, worries, and secrets truly are heard. Even when they disagree, loving partners listen to one another and acknowledge the right to authentic feelings. They pass the gift of acceptance back and forth, creating a climate for continued risk taking and growth.

Ruptures of trust occur regularly in relationships when partners shame, ignore, criticize, or lie. Hurt and anger multiply. People who have been hurt as children or in other relationships are very susceptible to carrying their pain into current relationships, thereby undermining them. Old fears, powerlessness, shame, hurt, and anger resurface—feelings that seem intolerable and unresolvable. People create protective shells for defense and escape as adaptations to the loss of trust.

Painful feelings can't stay covered forever, however. Consciously or subconsciously, new behaviors develop as ways to cope with the pain. Often addictions begin as a soothing way to escape from present reality.

War games that partners practice are frequently an element in an addictive pattern. These manipulations are unconscious attempts to regain power in the relationship. Money, sex, and children are frequent weapons that partners consciously or subconsciously use against each other. Money means power in our culture, so it is used as an unhealthy weapon in a hurting relationship. Eventually the partners may find themselves frozen in patterns of behavior that have become habitual:

Unfulfilled Intimacy Needs
(Foundations of Trust)

Safety
Honesty
Kindness
Respect

Ruptured Trust Patterns
(In Childhood, or a Past or Current Relationship)

Shaming
Ignoring
Criticizing
Lying

Fractured Relationships
(Characterized by Pain)

Fear
Powerlessness
Shame
Hurt
Anger

Protective Shell
(Pain Acted Out Against Self and Partner)

Addiction
Passive-aggressive behavior
Power struggle
Money used as weapon

The Deep Freeze
(Partners Frozen in Addictive, Passive-Aggressive Behavior)

Desperation
Numbness
Hopelessness
Depression
Rage

Effects of Money Issues

Resolution of money issues in current relationships begins with a personal inventory. The task requires work, honesty, grieving, and letting go of outmoded reactions to pain. People must understand what unresolved problems from the past each partner has brought into the relationship. Acknowledging the effects of parents' attitudes often begins the break from the past.

Money issues adversely affect relationships in a variety of ways. Review the following patterns that many couples unintentionally evolve, and decide which are familiar in your current life.

The Money-Master Game
I make all the money decisions in this family.

In some relationships, one person makes all of the money decisions, pays all of the bills, and controls how much money the other can spend, on what, and when.

Alice and John have been unable to find a way to resolve their money management conflicts. Alice wants some financial freedom but John insists that it's the man's place to make big money decisions.

He is willing to give her some personal money from the grocery budget, but she wants her own, separate checking account. John adamantly refuses.

The more Alice rebels, the tighter John clutches the purse strings. The one thing that Alice and John feel the same about is that they hurt a lot. Each feels that the pain is the partner's fault.

The Great Trade-Off Game

*I won't talk about your overspending and overeating
if you don't complain about my overworking.*

Partners agree to ignore one another's destructive behaviors in this pattern. Two hurting people, it has been said, cannot easily coexist. In the game of emotional trade-offs, both people are hurting, and each acts out escape behaviors without complaint about the other's excesses. They have developed a silent conspiracy and a mutual pattern of enabling that allows them to soothe themselves without confrontation.

John is a workaholic. He leaves home before the sun comes up and returns when Susan and the children are asleep. Even on Saturdays he sneaks off to the office, "just to check the mail," and returns seven or eight hours later. Susan spends and then overeats. She shops every day of the week. All of their joint credit cards, as well as the five cards in Susan's name that John doesn't know about, are at their limits of debt. She is hurt and feels rejected because he spends so little time with her. He feels betrayed because she appears to have turned into a materialistic, self-indulgent woman. Both remain silent for fear that they will be forced to examine their own behavior.

The Disability Game

*It's easier to fight about money than to uncover and talk about
what's really bothering me.*

Sometimes people transfer pain from other issues to money. Some things are so acutely painful, so deeply wounding, that people cannot bring themselves to deal with them. A seriously ill loved one, infertility, a death in the family, loss of employment—these are some of the crises that people avoid facing. Instead they act out their inner feelings by transferring them to someone or something else, as Homer did in his pain-filled marriage to Ruth. When she so much as thinks the word *money*, his rampages are so unbearable that she goes to any length to avoid money problems or discussions. Ruth and Homer are childless after five years of marriage. He became obsessed with money about three years ago, when he learned that he is infertile. He withdrew from Ruth then, without resolving his anger, guilt, and loss. Money diverted them from the grief that they never had discussed.

The Commitment Phobia Game

When I overfocus on money I don't have to make a commitment to you.

Overspending can be an excuse for avoiding commitment in other areas. A promotion with additional responsibilities and marriage are examples of commitments that demand a lot of effort. If people fear their inability to follow through, they may subconsciously or consciously cause their rejection and thereby avoid the risk of failure.

Bill is a young attorney who is almost phobic about commitment. Although he has dated Erma for four years, every time they talk about marriage, they end up in a money fight. She prides herself on her financial wisdom and ability to budget and save. He always has had some difficulty budgeting. Whenever commitment is mentioned, he goes on buying sprees that scare Erma to death. They both focus on money fights instead of wedding plans.

Bill feels horrible after these episodes and has promised Erma that he will learn to budget and plan better so they can be married. While she continues to hope, she feels that she's crazy to stay in the relationship . . . but he seems so sincere and loving after his spending sprees . . . maybe it will work out this time. Subconsciously Bill may use his money excesses to interrupt movement toward deeper levels of intimacy. Often commitment phobics underspend or overspend to avoid attending to the real issues.

The Benevolence Game

You can't be mad at me. After all, I'm just buying for others.

Buying for others may reflect feelings of unworthiness. If someone is disappointed in herself and feels that she never measures up, she may go on a perpetual quest to please others, trying to win approval through giving.

Ralph felt an anger as if his hands were tied whenever Sylvia overspent at the mall. He felt guilty and unloving when he complained about their dwindling cash reserve because Sylvia always reminded him that she bought for the family only because she loved them and wanted to make them happy. Besides, she found great bargains that were "too hard to pass up." After all, shopping was her way to show her love to everyone. How could he deny her this little pleasure?

Sylvia felt second best in their marriage because, unlike Ralph, she didn't have an interesting career. She was unwilling to risk more personal independence, rationalizing that her place was at home. She repressed her anger and personal disappointment by channeling it into buying for others. Ralph felt frustrated but too guilty to complain.

The World-Owes-Me Game

I didn't get what I needed as a child,
so don't expect me to be generous with you.

Stinginess reveals emotional deprivation. When one person in a relationship acts particularly stingy, withholding, and accusatory, past deprivation has caused a lack of trust in others and an expectation that people always will be a disappointment. The marriage of Ted and Alice is an example of this behavior. Their counseling began with her labeling him the family Scrooge.

Ted's Aunt Florence once described him as "rich in money but poor in spirit." His stinginess is a family joke that horrifies and embarrasses his wife and their children. Always quick to accuse Alice and the children of ingratitude and coldness when they ask for money, he controls the family budget with a vengeance. Alice is the primary target of his blame. He yells that she is greedy, money hungry, too indulgent with the children, and the cause of all of their marriage problems.

In childhood, Ted's basic emotional and security needs never were met. He feels a sense of entitlement—the world owes him compensation. He is always on guard and suspicious. He has learned to vent his rage and frustration toward his first family by punishing his current family. Because he is always looking for the worst, Ted finds the worst. He is on guard against the world and interprets his family's motives and actions as selfish, unappreciative, and unloving. Ted has a lot of money but little love in his life. His house is not a happy home but a place where everyone monitors every action to keep Ted calm. Extreme money deprivation and control in Ted's and Alice's relationship has caused grave damage to the whole family.

The Joneses Game

If you could just provide me with enough things, I might feel good about myself.

Overspending to "keep up with the Joneses" may mask deep feelings of emptiness resulting from early deprivation. The glamorous clothes and status cars may serve only as a facade.

Eloise grew up in a family that never seemed to have enough to go around. School was difficult for Eloise because she lived on the fringe of the "in" crowd. Without designer clothes, jewelry, and a pretty house, she felt she couldn't compete. By the time she was twelve she firmly equated money with happiness. Dick married Eloise right after law school, and they both became involved in the pursuit of the "good life." No matter how much he earned, they never seemed to be able to save. Keeping up with the Joneses had in fact become their marital vocation.

Dick eventually grew tired and frightened of the cycle they were in but felt powerless to interrupt the pattern of their relationship. Eloise couldn't understand why he didn't love her enough to make as much money as her friend Kitty's husband.

Eloise never has acknowledged and mourned the feelings of deprivation and separation she felt while growing up. She continues to try and fill the empty space in her life, finding that the more things she has, the emptier she feels. She might have acted in the same manner even if her material needs had been satisfied in childhood, however, for the same pattern occurs when deeper emotional needs are not met.

The Spend, Don't Spend Game

You buy what you want. I can just do without.

The double messages in this game come from personal ambivalence and the need to control others.

Doug always encourages Kathy to spend money and buy the things she likes but consistently denies himself new clothing and other nice things. He says, "I can't buy that for myself—it's too expensive. Besides, I really don't need it. My shoes are only two years old; they'll be great after I get them resoled." Kathy does spend money but always feels guilty afterward.

Doug's double messages reflect his unresolved feelings about his own value. Although he wants Kathy to have nice things, he feels angry when she accepts. He also wants nice things but hasn't learned how to nurture himself without guilt.

The Russian Roulette Game

Let's pretend the scalding water we're standing in is lukewarm.

Spend today with tomorrow's money. In this game people spend money they don't have because they believe their ship will come in any day. When large sums of money don't land in their laps, they say, "Next time!"

Cole keeps Tina and himself living on the edge by spending today against money that might come in tomorrow. Life feels like a daring game to Tina. She longs to believe Cole's promises but is afraid because she has been disappointed often about "big deals" that somehow never materialized. Tina is beginning to wonder why she is so willing to spend money based on Cole's promises. Both of them have stopped opening bills, as if to say that they don't exist if Cole and Tina don't see them. Last week the electricity was disconnected because she had neglected to pay the bill. The higher their debts stack up, the more the couple spend, and the more numb they become.

Cole is not honest and objective about his financial situation. He minimizes and denies his problems, promising that things will get better when the "big deal comes in." Tina has been drawn into his delusional money games. They both live on the edge instead of risking an honest look at their situation.

The Family Feud Game

You act just like my mother when it comes to money.

Some people transfer onto their partners the desire to control one or both parents. A child who lived her life wishing her mom or dad would act differently may impose those wishes on her mate when she is grown.

Mary Lou hates to spend money on fun, but her husband, Tim, acts just like her mother, always wanting to have fun and spend money. Tim always plans trips and other "escapes from reality" instead of saving, and nothing makes Mary Lou madder. How did she ever marry someone so frivolous that he can't get his priorities straight? Mary Lou is glad she's practical like her father. Whoever heard of a family needing a vacation each year and a night out every weekend? If it weren't for her good judgment, they wouldn't have so much money in the bank. She wonders why Tim doesn't feel as thrilled as she does about their savings account.

Mary Lou grew up in a family with unresolved intimacy and power issues. Mary identified with her strict father, feeling that her mother's foolish need to enjoy life was wasteful.

The Hide-and-Seek Game

He'll never know if I just cheat a little on our budget.

A compulsive spender may avoid a partner's confrontation by lying, scheming, and deceiving. The result is a parent-child relationship between two adults.

Mary bought new clothes that she and her husband Pete could not afford. She told Pete that they were a birthday gift from her parents. She wrote checks to the grocery store, but instead of using the money for food, she shopped at the mall. Pete believed that they had an unusually high food bill.

On the occasions when he caught Mary in a lie, Pete couldn't get too mad because he thought it was rather cute. She was relieved, but not completely. People took Pete seriously. They listened to him and asked his opinions abut politics and current events. But Mary noticed that people merely smiled sweetly at her. Even when she does something that seriously injures the marriage and the trust it's built on, she still isn't taken seriously.

The Even-the-Score Game
Watch what you do or I'll get back at you by spending.

Overspending can be a device for revenge. It can say, I'll show you, in a very loud and unmistakable fashion.

Larry discovered that money was the great "get back" in his and June's relationship. He'd show her he was tired of her moods, her ups and downs. Once when she wasn't attentive to him, he bought a fancy mower and mulcher to get even. After all, he was the man in the family, and he could decide what to do with their money. June was devastated. He said she knew why he bought it, but June knew only that she felt slapped and betrayed. She cried herself to sleep that night and moved away from Larry to her side of the bed.

These people are playing hidden anger games with each other. Instead of owning and working through their hurts and marital problems as they occur, they avoid the real issues by staying caught in the drama of money fights.

The Great Checkbook Game
I'm sorry I forgot to record the check. I'm not as good at details as you are.

Victims and persecutors keep poor money records. Couples can become entangled in a patterned fight about the checking account because of poor communication in their relationship. When they have not cultivated the skill and confidence to talk openly with one another, they often do so in gestures, often expressed in the family checkbook.

Tony and Margaret have a joint checking account. She records all of the checks she writes, but he "forgets" to record some of his. The account is overdrawn and a check bounces. Margaret is enraged, but Tony doesn't understand what all the fuss is about and promises again to record all of his transactions. Despite his guarantees, however, the pattern repeats.

Tony feels trapped and controlled in the marriage. He feels stripped of his identity but can't say so in words. In her anger, Margaret pressures Tony to conform to her ways by reprimanding him about the checkbook. Her efforts to control him make Tony feel increasingly henpecked. He fights back unconsciously through the checkbook.

The Blame Game

Someday you'll change the way you feel about money and we'll be happy.

Some couples conduct a game in which one tries to make the other feel crazy and intimidated enough to allow the abuse.

Paul and Mindy have the same argument over and over again. Mindy is sick and tired of money problems. She can't take the children to the pediatrician because they never paid the last bill. She can't invite friends to dinner because they can't afford it. Mindy has a full-time job, but Paul works only sporadically. Occasionally, when she gets the courage to bring up the money thing, Paul explodes, accusing Mindy of being spoiled and gauche for talking about the "M" word. He makes all purchase decisions. Although Mindy resents his reserving such power for himself, she allows it in order to keep the peace. They live far below their financial potential, which suits Paul but wears Mindy out. After their money arguments, she feels ashamed and dismissed, but she can't figure out just what happened. Paul feels unappreciated and betrayed. He spends a lot of time creating problems for Mindy to dwell on. She spends most of her time trying to fix the family and all of its problems

Afraid of Paul's reactions, Mindy walks on eggs when he is home. As a child she learned to be seen and not heard. She continues to suffer from low self-esteem, which has been undermined further by Paul's outbursts. She waits for him magically to change and make her happy. Paul also suffers from low self-esteem, which results in his need to control, call all the shots, and keep Mindy subservient, lest she develop a mind of her own and decide she doesn't need (or want or love) him anymore. Money is the perfect device to deflect attention from core abuse issues that seem too painful to address.

The Silver Spoon Game

I don't have to be fiscally responsible because I was raised with wealth and am entitled to special privileges.

If one or both partners come from a wealthy background, they may have difficulty accepting a lower standard of living when they become independent. An attitude of entitlement destroys the potential to create one's own abundance.

Anne was raised with domestic help who cared for the home and children. She never thought about prices and charged anything that pleased her to her father's account. When she went to college she majored in enjoyment, paying little attention to preparing herself for a career.

Anne married Michael, who had been similarly reared. She thought she didn't care that his field would not pay well. Michael and Anne soon discovered that their new lifestyle would require more than vows and good intentions. They quickly got into trouble with check writing; both felt entitled to certain things whether or not they could afford them. They were indignant when creditors called or stores refused to extend additional credit to them. They thought their landlord was abusive because he demanded two months' overdue rent. Anne refused to work because the jobs she qualified for were not impressive.

Both Michael and Anne entered the adult world with no practical training. Anne felt like a failure because she was domestically inept; she wanted to stay at home and raise children, but without training or money she was frustrated. Michael also felt like a failure because he compulsively spent more than he had, and he continually had to defend himself to angry lenders, landlords, and his wife. They blamed each other to mask their true feelings of shame, embarrassment, and failure.

Survey of Money Issues in Relationships

Relationships seem to relax when the money issues are squarely evaluated. They may prove to be a smoke screen for deeper problems of trust and security that can't be seen in the heat of money games. Even though confrontation of the real weaknesses in a relationship may be difficult and painful initially, honest self-knowledge always turns out to be a good thing. Sometimes people spend years building mountains of money entanglements that take time to unravel. Couples must be willing to survey and expose their parts in money games in order to reveal the deeper issues. After they have surveyed their histories separately, they can begin more easily a mutual dialogue.

The following money survey helps couples get at the issues that underlie their money problems. Which money games apply to you and your current relationship as well as your relationship with your first family?

Who are the chief players in this money game?

_____

_____

_____

_____

How is the game played (a typical situation)?

_____

_____

_____

_____

_____

What is your part in the game?

_____

_____

_____

_____

What might be some deeper feelings and issues behind the game?

_____

_____

_____

_____

What are some of the unmet needs in your relationship that this game expresses?

_____

_____

_____

_____

_____

_____

What can you do to become honest and to change your part in this money game? (Be specific.)

_____

_____

_____

_____

_____

_____

_____

_____

What might stop you from making and following through on a commitment to change?

_____

_____

_____

_____

_____

_____

10

Families and Money Maneuvers

Most parents and grandparents want their children to grow up with solid money management skills. They want to provide well for their kids without doing for them what is healthy for them to do on their own. They want their adult children to be financially independent but at the same time wouldn't mind offering occasional financial assistance if they can afford it and the child does not abuse their help. Despite their best intentions, some parents and grandparents transmit harmful money messages to their children. In the name of love they inadvertently accomplish the opposite of their intentions.

Don's Story

Don and Louise were married in 1956. Since they were fresh out of college and just starting out in the world, Don's parents offered them the use of a house they owned and had rented out for years. They said that Don and Louise didn't have to pay rent while they saved for a down payment on a house of their own. Then the first baby came, and Don was between jobs, so his parents supported the new family while Don looked for a position that suited him.

When Don had been in the Indian Explorers Boys Club at the age of nine, he and the other children sold leather key cases that they had assembled and decorated in authentic Indian designs to raise funds for a wilderness trip. Don's mother took the entire box of key cases. "It's silly for you to spend time going door to door," she said, "when I can sell them all for you today at my ladies' club meeting."

In high school, when the neighbors hired him to water the garden and house plants while they were vacationing, Don forgot all of his duties. The plants died. His parents scolded him and then replaced the plants that hadn't survived the neglect.

Now Don was out of work at Christmastime and had no money for gifts, so his parents gave him a loan. He bought a brooch for his wife, who worked at a full-time job to make ends meet. Finally Don found work, lots of work—one job right after the other. Three more babies arrived. The arguments about money, in-laws, and pain escalated to the point of divorce in 1966.

The only snag in the divorce of Don and Louise was the attorney's fees. Of course they had no money, so Don's parents wrote the checks, as always.

The Best Intentions

During Don's childhood, his parents clearly had intended the best for him. When he forgot to water the neighbor's plants they eagerly went about setting things right again. They just wanted to help their son out of a jam and restore to the neighbors the plants they had lost. The message they hoped to send to Don was:
We love you and want to help you with a d difficult situation.

The message Don received was:
When you don't fulfill your obligations, no consequences will follow and someone will always rescue you.

When Don's mother sold his key cases, she believed she was sending this message:
I love you, so I'll make things easy for you.

The messages Don received were some or all of these:
I don't think you are capable; otherwise I would allow you to succeed yourself.

You are different from the other kids who are out there going door to door.

Your creations are not beautiful enough to sell, so I'll take them off your hands.

When Don was married and living rent-free in his parents' house, they believed they were sending this message:

We love you and wish to express our support for your new marriage, so we are giving this gift to you.

The messages Don heard were:

We don't think you can be a good provider, so we'll provide what you cannot.

We think of you as a child who can't take care of himself; you deserve to be taken care of.

When his parents helped Don to buy the Christmas brooch for Louise, they meant to say:

We love you—Merry Christmas.

But the message he received was:

We don't think you're capable of meeting your obligations as a husband, so we'll fulfill them for you.

Don's parents could have suggested that he simply get a job to tide his family over until he found the one he was looking for. By suggesting this alternative, his parents would have communicated their belief in Don and his ability to be a functioning, independent person.

Louise contributed to the scenario by assuming the role of sole provider and full-time homemaker while Don was neither, thereby delivering some messages of her own. She may have meant to say, Honey, I love you and our babies, so I'm willing to make sacrifices in order to help make ends meet. Don may have drawn the conclusion, They all think I'm incapable.

This point comes up to show how family dynamics work, not to blame Louise, who must cope with the consequences to herself and their children of Don's lack of motivation. Louise is caught between the proverbial rock and hard place. As in other families where responsibility is disproportionate, her excessive effort permits Don to persist in doing less than he could and should. If she does *not* do her share and Don's as well, she and her children lack the necessities. She fills the vacuum that his paralysis creates, staving off the crisis that the whole family would suffer otherwise. Her dilemma is acutely painful, with neither option tolerable.

Don's parents and Louise unintentionally became his enablers. Enablers are generally loving and caring people who truly want to give of themselves and help others. The problem is that they create dependency and enable their children or spouses to avoid taking some of the responsibility for their own lives. Often they have little notion of where they end and another person begins. This phenomenon is particularly common with "boomerang kids." These young people have gone into the world as adults but return to live with their parents. Often they bring their children. This situation presents problems that parents and children must resolve. Solutions are not always obvious, however, as parents attempt to offer caring support without enabling and fostering dependence.

If the child willingly is working toward financial independence, his parents may comfortably offer proper support. If, however, the child is not trying hard, the parent must decide, painfully sometimes, on the response that would be healthiest for the child. Yet it is difficult to stop helping someone you love when he won't help himself. Parents should be aware that financial enabling is destructive in the long run, even though it may seem to meet some short-term needs of the enabler.

Parents, Money Motives, and the Consequences

- Parents may want to feel needed. They keep their children financially dependent so they won't leave home.

- Parents may want to absolve themselves of guilt by using money to make up for their adult children's unhappy childhoods. They attempt to re-parent with excessive financial assistance.

- Parents who have been victimized recreate their role by allowing their adult children to take advantage of them. They use personal sacrifice to elicit sympathy and gratitude.

- Parents with intimacy issues find it more comfortable to use money instead of hugs to express feelings.

It is critical that parents examine their motives and ask honestly what message their money behavior sends to their children. Sometimes parents send conflicting messages to their children, attaching either too much meaning or too little significance to money. The child grows to value or undervalue it.

Mary Jane grew up in just such confusion about money. Her father was an alcoholic and her mother was depressed. Usually just one step ahead of eviction from their apartment, they never had money for "extras." Whenever a neighborhood kid received a new bike or wagon, Mary Jane's father said, "Well, well, well, they just had to get a brand new bike. Spoiled rotten, that's what those kids are!" At the same time, her folks had sophisticated tastes. When they did buy something, it was always the best. Mary Jane remembers finding rare exotic Easter eggs in her Easter basket, but the phone was disconnected owing to no payment just a few days later. Although her father was drunk and explosive most of the time, her parents argued not about drinking but about money. They used the subject to skirt around the issue of alcoholism.

When Mary Jane did have something nice, she felt embarrassed and selfish, as though everyone who saw her in her new outfit were eyeing her critically. She wore the new outfit with cheap earrings or something torn and soiled, to relieve her guilt. She was glad about the first little ding in her brand new car, so she finally could enjoy it. Spending binges almost destroyed her life. "I got so far into debt I became suicidal. And I always had this conflict, this confusion. I wanted nice things; when I didn't have nice clothes or a decent car, I was sad and felt that I was on the lowest rung in society." Now Mary Jane is in recovery and attends ACoA (Adult Children of Alcoholics) as well as DA meetings.

Grandparents

Financial emancipation is more complicated than ever for today's youth. The job market requires more technical skills and college experience than was demanded of past generations. Health care costs have rocketed, and housing costs now absorb a greater proportion of an individual's paycheck than in years past. Even with two incomes, today's young adults find it increasingly difficult to buy homes in the neighborhoods where they were raised. The number of people on welfare steadily increases and recession has wracked the economy.

For all of these reasons, adult children are returning home in droves. According to the 1990 Census, one of nine adults between ages twenty-five and thirty-four resided then in a parent's home. With the additional problems of drugs, alcohol, dysfunctional relationships, and other life-destroying factors, our society is turning out adults who are financially dependent on their parents. And these adults often come calling with children in tow.

What can a grandparent do? Grandchildren confuse the question of how much, if any, financial assistance one should offer. Ellen's daughter, Sue, had a little girl named Tammy. In accordance with the rules of the daycare center where she was enrolled, Tammy could not play outside at recess because she didn't have boots. Ellen ached to buy her granddaughter the boots she needed. On the other hand, she was angry at Sue for not providing the boots in the first place. Sue had a history of job hopping and spending money on extras rather than essentials. Sue was acting irresponsibly with money and had come to believe that she was entitled to financial assistance ever since her divorce. She became very angry at the mere suggestion that she might put more effort into working and providing for her child.

Ellen knew she was rescuing Sue from responsibility every time she provided something for Tammy that Sue herself could have afforded had she not spent money entertaining or buying clothes for herself. She made a deal with Sue: "I'll buy Tammy a pair of boots if you repay me by cleaning out the attic." Of course, Ellen also had to plan her response should Sue test her and refuse the arrangement.

The conflicting emotions grandparents suffer when asked to help their adult children financially can be excruciating, as Ellen's story shows. In a perfect world, adult children would always be hardworking and responsible people so help could be a warm experience of bonding with one's children and grandchildren. When financial assistance feels uncomfortable, it is advisable to get some outside help to assess the health of the situation. The profound love a parent feels for children and grandchildren can cloud their view. A counselor or other grand-parents who have dealt successfully with a similar situation can help one judge whether money is obstructing the financial responsibility of the young. While a grandparent wants financial assistance to ben-efit a grandchild, it actually may hurt the child in the long run if the help keeps the parent dependent.

Money Can Fix Everything

Look around the room at a suburban juvenile court to see many young people being defended by their parents' attorneys. Most of these young people will pay little, if anything, toward their defense. Afterward they will resume their lives, some court time having been their only incon-venience. Most will learn the following lessons from the adults in court:

- Money can fix everything.
- There's always a way to beat the system.
- Rules and laws are for other people.
- Mom and Dad's actions say that they approve of stealing, van-dalism, or shoplifting, since they pay the consequences.

While the parents believe they are helping their children, they may do more harm than good. One of the most difficult tasks for parents is allowing children to suffer the natural consequences of their actions. Those who do so generally enjoy watching their kids become respon-sible and independent adults. Those who don't may create social infants—adults who remain irresponsible and dependent on others.

Guidelines for Healthy Financial Assistance

Not all assistance from parents and grandparents is harmful. Some adult children are consistently responsible. They meet their obliga-tions and honor agreements. They pay back debt as promised and take control of their financial future. These are the people who may bene-fit from occasional financial assistance. For example, Richard wanted to go back to college as an adult. He had saved some money to pay for half of his expenses. He had borrowed money from his father in the past and repaid it on schedule. He had earned passing marks when he was in school before and demonstrated good work and study habits. His father felt comfortable offering to lend Richard the other half of his tuition.

Richard's sister, Karen, needed money, too, for the purchase of a car. She had been in her current job only two months. She already had two outstanding loans with her father that she was not paying back reliably, and she hadn't put up any of her own money toward the auto down payment. Her father refused Karen's request. Like any self-respecting thwarted sibling, Karen cried foul play and accused Dad of playing favorites. He quietly explained that he would be happy to lend her half of the down payment after she had paid back the first loan and saved the other half of the down payment herself. Dad tossed the ball back into her court, giving Karen the gift of independence with a sweet reward waiting for her at the end.

Here are some general guidelines for healthy financial assistance:
• Reserve loans for adult children with a history of fiscal responsibility.

• Draw up a contract that specifies the agreement.

• Ask yourself whether you can lend money without emotional strings. If the family historically has used money as a weapon or a controlling device, financial deals are unwise.

• Judge each situation differently and look at the overall picture. A request for a very small amount of money may seem unimportant, but if the recipient constantly borrows a little here, a little there, a wise parent might reconsider. Wisdom works the other way, too. Sometimes a request seems out of line until the overall picture demonstrates good faith, ability to pay back, and genuine need.

• Financial assistance is unwise if unresolved money problems stand between the two parties. Outstanding loans, money disagreements, and differences of opinion about money in general signal the need for an agreement to avoid financial deals.

- Assistance that puts undue strain on the lender is not advised. If you can't afford it, don't do it.

- Money gifts should be given without strings attached. A parent can't give a son a hundred dollars for his birthday and expect him to honor the unwritten contract that says he must never argue with his father now that this "gift" has been bestowed.

- Under most circumstances, parents should decline to lend or give money to adult children who have outstanding debts with them already, particularly if they have not repaid them as promised.

- A parent who lends money to children should do so in good spirit. Both parties should feel good about it.

- If an adult child is recovering from compulsive spending, parents must not talk them into actions that are not part of their recovery program.

Double Messages

College-bound students commonly leave home with more than just their stereo systems and suitcases. They also may take along spoken or unspoken parental money messages, like Go to college, but we can't afford it. A parent's delivering such a contradiction is like his saying, Wash the car, but don't get it wet. Yet it's what lots of college kids hear every year.

Suzanne's parents encouraged her to go to college. They helped her with her application and were excited when she finally was accepted. She went to a relatively inexpensive state college and made the dean's list the first semester. When she came home, she was marched over to her father's desk, where he had kept a file on her and the college expenses. "Your college expenses," he said, "are killing this family."

Peggy remembers coming home for spring break and seeing her mother attend a wedding in worn, outdated shoes. Asked why she hadn't bought new ones, she said she couldn't afford them because Peggy's school tuition was so high. On the one hand, Peggy was praised for her college career, but on the other hand, she was ashamed of it.

Tom's parents agreed to pay his college tuition but only if he chose a lucrative vocation, not necessarily one that he felt he was suited for. He wanted to teach, but his parents wouldn't allow that because "teaching doesn't pay." Tom received two messages: We're behind you one hundred percent . . . but not all the time.

Parents and students need to discuss *all* financial details regarding college education, covering who is responsible for which expense and the "hidden" emotional costs (resentments, sacrifices, and anger). Parents need to discuss their expectations and strive to create a trusting atmosphere and healthy boundaries so that both parents and children feel comfortable airing opinions, feelings, and concerns.

Dealing with the Inner Child

Parents and grandparents can identify their own unmet childhood needs as a first step toward understanding and responsibility for current behavior. Then they can satisfy those needs appropriately, thereby improving their chances to meet the needs of their children. (If I didn't feel safe as a child, I probably still don't feel safe as an adult.) In recovery, they can build a foundation of trust and give up the compulsive behavior. Recognition of self-destructive attitudes and their origins is not to blame their parents but to claim responsibility for healing. What matters is not what happened in the past but what they now have learned. Informed parents and grandparents can avoid passing on their destructive experiences.

CHAPTER

11

Grieving—A Journey through Pain and Sorrow

The admission that some things in life are beyond our control permits one to feel and grieve the losses of yesterday and today. Grief reveals the pain that was buried by compulsive spending and other self-medicating money behaviors.

Ginny, whose story began in chapter 2, has some serious losses in her life. People who are married to alcoholics tend to lose respect for the person they once held in high esteem, and they lose security. They lose the dream of a joyful and intimate relationship with their spouses. Often they lose money, friends, the trust and respect of their children, confidence and faith, spiritual well-being, and sanity.

But suppose Ginny divorced Noel? Would she stop spending compulsively? Noel is probably not at the root of Ginny's spending problem. Her wounds go deeper into her past than the few years she's been married to Noel. As a child she learned that she wasn't good enough as she was and saw that her stepfather was ashamed of her. Her mother had taught Ginny to stuff her feelings, not to express and deal with them. She learned not to feel. When she was grown, Noel appealed to her (his alcoholism was not yet apparent) because his cold and withholding nature was familiar. He was often very warm and loving during their courtship but had an aura of danger that felt comfortable.

Some people fall in love with those most likely to disappoint them. The scariest thing about that inclination is the fact that usually the partner does nothing overt to exhibit the potential for pain. But if both were victims as children, they may repeat the same familiar patterns as adults and become victims, victimizers, or both. Ginny does not cause Noel's drinking any more than Noel causes Ginny's spending, but together they perpetuate a painful family system. Both Noel and Ginny have losses and hurts to mourn. Both are in pain, and both need to heal.

Grief confronts us with reality from which we cannot hide. An integral part of life, grief heals because it allows us to know ourselves as we really are in our fragility, beauty, and humanity. No human being is immune to loss. People connect grief with losses in death, but more and more acceptable is the view that grief is present in almost any loss of something valued, whether it be great or small. Losses may be tangible and concrete: illness, unemployment, or the death of a beloved. Other losses are emotional: loss of self-esteem, friendship, or trust in a significant relationship. In recovery, people experience several stages of grief and loss.

Shame

Children and teenagers are unable to separate themselves easily from others' actions. Youngsters who are abused by parents lack the emotional maturity to understand that they did not cause the abuse. They may internalize the experience and develop unhealthy shame, thinking, If my parent treats me badly, I must be bad; if my own mother or father doesn't protect me, then I must deserve this abuse. When caused by deprivation or abuse, shame does not fade away into an unpleasant childhood memory.

Guilt

Guilt refers to behavior: I feel guilty for overspending today. It is a functional response, like an alarm that goes off and forces a close look at personal actions. Shame, in contrast, is not functional. It speaks about who and what people are. Someone who says "I'm ashamed of you" is talking about the person, not the person's behavior. Shame is unhealthy when it manifests itself in perfectionism, acting out, and addictions and compulsions. These behaviors temporarily relieve feelings of shame, but the relief is short-lived; people begin to feel new shame about their compulsive behavior, and the cycle continues.

As you begin to grieve for your losses and disappointments, you will come to recognize the unhealthy shame living within you. Once you recognize its existence you will be able to acknowledge and rid yourself of it. You can't get rid of something you don't even know you have.

Initial Anger

As you begin to uncover and expose your unhealthy shame you will feel anger about real and imagined hurts. When people stop spending compulsively, they find themselves sitting face to face with the things that really drive them without camouflage or escape. They may express their feelings sharply and inappropriately. When irritants pop up, the source of initial anger may be hard to identify and its outcome may be misdirected at your children and dog. Honesty challenges you to look deeper and sort out the issues by thinking, talking, and writing about the source of your real anger and hurt. Knowing what you're angry about gives you the power to be assertive and face the persons or situations that anger you. You shouldn't express your anger in order to change another person, but only to change yourself. Even if you feel victimized, it is still your challenge to change. If you don't, the anger continues to grow, hurting you far more than the person you're angry with.

When Ginny mourned the loss of her father, she faced her suppressed anger at both parents. She was angry that her mother hadn't allowed her to cry and feel pain. Both parents had deceived her about the critical nature of her father's illness. Then her stepfather never had loved her unconditionally. Once Ginny allowed herself to acknowledge her anger and hurt, it no longer controlled her.

Legitimate anger does not give recovering people the right to throw temper tantrums. Their right is merely to express how they feel in a safe way. If they feel uneasy speaking directly to the objects of their anger, they can express themselves to others who do seem safe. Honesty about their anger takes them further along in the grieving process.

The other side of the anger stage for recovering people is their dealing with others' anger toward them. Surely Ginny's husband Noel is angry about her spending. Others' anger usually focuses on one or a few things and rarely is generalized. If your neighbor is mad because you promised to go somewhere with her and then reneged, she's mad about something you did; she's not mad that you exist! You don't have to bake a plate of cookies for her and baby-sit her children for a month. You do not need to move. Compulsive people often see things in black and white. They fail to see the gray areas, those areas that are not all good or bad, not all right or wrong. Good friends sometimes disappoint each other. Spouses may be angry and yet love one another at the same time.

If you were raised in a dysfunctional home, you may have learned to view the world in black and white terms. Anger was a very frightening emotion, one to be avoided at all costs. Small mistakes often precipitated family blowups. Healthy people in healthy relationships feel, express, and release their anger. It is not a weapon or a controlling device; nor do they suppress it and allow it to eat away at them. They feel safe enough to own it and deal with it. As money addicts grieve for past and present losses, anger surfaces when they least expect it. When it does it is imperative that they deal with it and not just let it accumulate.

Depression

Anger frightens many people. If not identified and expressed, it may turn into depression. People in this state feel listless and lack energy, zest, or motivation. For the overspender, the temptation to spend supersedes the need to talk, write, read, or exercise, strategies that might ease the depression. A person whose depression persists, accompanied by a pattern of changes in eating, sleeping, or regular activities, should consult a mental health professional and a doctor.

Some depression is normal. All people feel it from time to time, and it is to be expected when money addicts cease to abuse money. Healing often hurts, but the end result is confidence, serenity, and contentment that feels wonderful!

Fear

Money addicts may be afraid to stop their compulsive behavior and face the realities of their lives. Fear may seem like a monster, always walking just behind them, ready to pounce. The only cure for fear is to face it. Running away will not help those in recovery. Confronting fear is not nearly as painful as running away. If poverty is a fear, can it be disguised by fake affluence bought on credit?

Scott feared that he would be poor. He never fit in and felt embarrassed and ashamed. The more he spent on clothes, cars, and vacations, the more he reassured himself that he was not poor. Scott also was overweight and obsessed with finding clothes that hid his bulk and were flattering. He felt secure in the knowledge that he had clothes for any occasion. Now he says that he didn't run from his fear of his eating problem; he rode away from it in a very expensive car. In recovery, Scott faced his fears. Now, strong and confident, he believes he can handle whatever comes his way.

Validation

When you recognize your shame, anger, depression, and fear, you are saying to yourself that you count. All of your feelings do indeed exist, and they are a part of you. Recovering people recognize that their feelings are normal. This knowledge affirms them.

Early in his recovery, Michael felt undeserving of anything nice. He felt that his spending had ruined all chances of his ever feeling worthwhile again. But he kept attending DA meetings, reading the literature, and following his spending plan. He faced the feelings that his compulsive spending had numbed. After a while, he noticed some "strange sensations," "little bursts of something." A fellow DA member asked, "Like bursts of happiness maybe?" Michael laughed and said, "Yeah, that's what it is."

During recovery, those bursts of happiness pick up speed and come more frequently as time passes. They make way for confidence and feelings of value.

Hope

When money addicts deal with their feelings, they usually discover that they hold up better than they had expected. Once recognized, those feelings become easier to release. They lose their power. In recovery, therefore, people feel hopeful. The further along in recovery, the more optimistic they become. When money addicts attend Debtors Anonymous meetings they see others just like themselves, people who laugh and enjoy life and demonstrate by example that recovery builds joy.

Acceptance

Acceptance involves acknowledging the reality of past experiences and believing that you cannot change anyone but yourself.

Ginny's husband Noel drinks too much. Ginny needs to come to terms with the fact that she can't change Noel. She must accept the fact that he is responsible for his actions and she for hers. If she is ever to work through her grief and other phases of recovery, she must accept her childhood losses and her current spending. She will accept the things she cannot change and accept responsibility for changing the things she can. Along with acceptance comes relief. Acceptance initially sounds like submission, like giving up, but it feels more like relief. Addicts are unaware of the emotional toll and energy the fight against demons takes until it stops.

Personal Freedom

Money addicts may accept the fact that their spending is compulsive and that they have no control over others, but they often remain enmeshed in unhealthy relationships.

If you lie awake nights brooding about your stepmother's weird behavior, if you put your own life on hold in order to help everyone else, then you have become enmeshed. You may no longer respond like an individual but instead function more like a gear in someone else's watch, moving only in reaction to the watch's action. If you are involved in an abusive relationship, you may need to seek professional counseling to move you along the road to freedom.

Individual personal freedom calls for the establishment of personal boundaries. These boundaries declare personal ownership of self. You are not a part of another person. When someone feels personally free, other people's problems or behavior cannot dominate her thoughts. She knows where she ends and others begin; she is not part of somebody else, wrapped up in another's drama. A person with firm boundaries feels whole independently of others.

Good-bye Spending, Hello Feelings

A Personal History

Learning healthy spending patterns will quickly bring you face to face with your feelings. If you are using money to numb yourself, removal of that screen will quickly reveal what's really been going on inside. Honesty about money is a big risk and challenge. If someone is in a relationship in which money problems cover deeper issues, the relationship patterns and balance of power shifts when one partner begins to change. Even healthy changes can threaten a troubled relationship. Yet honestly facing difficulties challenges people to make changes for the better.

Complete the following personal history to assess your history and attitudes regarding money. This profile builds on and enlarges the information you discovered in chapter 9, the survey of money issues in relationships. Answer the questions as honestly as possible. Write your thoughts without changing or monitoring your responses.

What images or pictures come to mind when you think of the word *money?*

What were your family's attitudes about money?

Mom: _____

_____

_____

_____

Dad: _____

_____

_____

_____

Others (siblings, aunts, uncles, grandparents, family friends): ____

_____

_____

_____

You as a child: _____

_____

_____

_____

_____

What payoff do you get from the money games in your life?

_____

_____

_____

_____

Have you ever used money to punish yourself or others?

_____

_____

_____

_____

Have you ever used money to reward yourself or others?

_____

_____

_____

_____

_____

Are you willing to change your attitudes and rules about money now? Why or why not?

_____

_____

_____

_____

_____

_____

_____

What do you think might change in your life if you changed attitudes and rules about money?

_____

_____

_____

_____

What would you have to give up? What current and past losses would you need to mourn?

_____

_____

_____

_____

_____

_____

What would you gain?

_____

_____

_____

_____

_____

_____

What scares you about changing your relationship with money?

_____

_____

_____

_____

_____

_____

_____

List the specific money problems and areas you want to begin working on.

_____

_____

_____

_____

_____

_____

_____

_____

_____

_____

_____

_____

_____

_____

_____

_____

_____

_____

_____

_____

_____

_____

Part Three

The Full Heart

CHAPTER

12

Uncovering Denial and Other Smoke Screens

Denial and other coping mechanisms are defensive smoke screens that temporarily camouflage the risk, pain, and consequences of unhealthy behavior. Coping mechanisms help people to avoid the reality that compulsive behaviors relieve, the downs of life as well as its ups. As these behaviors start to harm money addicts, denial dulls awareness, protecting them from clearly seeing their excesses. Coping mechanisms are subconscious shields that cover the truth.

Denial

Joe's spending frightened his fiancée, Dee. She saw the pile of late notices and letters from creditors on his kitchen table. When she inquired, he said that credit card companies expect you to be late.

Later, after dinner at a restaurant, Joe presented his credit card to the waitress. She brought it back saying, "It didn't go through."

"No problem," Joe said. He tried two more bank cards before number three finally was accepted. When Dee expressed her concern Joe said it was no big deal. "It's the American way!" he said.

Joe used denial to shield himself from the reality of his spending.

The coping mechanism of denial is also a mask for Joe's shame about spending that is out of control and about his not having a profession like all of the men in Dee's family. When she suggests that they stay in rather than go out and spend money, Joe feels mortified.

Shame is the hardest of feelings to bear. It dampens spirits and causes people to discount their goodness. Denial and other coping mechanisms initially seem to protect people from shame about themselves and their actions, especially behavior that hurts themselves or others. The more people spend, the more ashamed they feel and the more they use denial to numb this reality. They can't begin to plan financial solvency as long as they deny their compulsive spending.

Other Unconscious Smoke Screens

Denial manifests itself in combination with other coping mechanisms. Here are some of the more common themes.

Devaluation

Someone who is not doing well financially and emotionally may devalue or put down others in order to cover up his own guilt and fear about money abuse. One who criticizes others while oblivious to one's own faults unfairly hurts others in an especially painful way. Recovering money addicts say that they devalued people close to them by being excessively negative, critical, and demeaning. Doing so, they subconsciously distracted themselves from their own precarious house of cards.

Projection

This coping mechanism attributes one's thoughts or feelings to others. A woman might tell her husband that he seems to be angry, when in reality she feels angry toward him. Projection clouds issues she would rather not deal with.

Displacement

Displaced feelings are directed toward the wrong object. If a man is ashamed and angry at himself for a spending binge, he may deny and displace this anger by coming home and yelling at the children for not having picked up their toys. Displacement confuses everyone in a compulsive spender's life.

Repression

The unconscious refusal to allow strong feelings to surface is another coping mechanism, repression. The strategy never works for long; the strong feelings come back indirectly. A compulsive spender who is afraid to show anger directly to her husband, for example, may buy him a shirt style he dislikes and be surprised at his reaction. Repression causes money addicts to lose touch with their true feelings.

The story of Ginny in chapters 2 and 8 makes it clear that she represses strong feelings from her childhood. As a little girl, she was abandoned by her father when he died. She was forbidden to express her grief. Since mourning was never allowed to occur, the grief never left her; it just crouched in a corner of her psyche, waiting to pounce. Ginny kept it caged by focusing her energies on her spending and the resulting worries.

Alongside the grief that breathes and lives and waits for a reckoning are a host of other likely feelings: vulnerability, incompetence, shame, anger, and fear of abandonment. By focusing her time and resources on money, the acquisition of things, and financial manipulations, the money addict delays confronting repressed feelings, pushing them further and further from consciousness.

Compensation

Compensation is a way to counterbalance defects. A woman may feel inadequate as a wife and partner. She may then compensate for her feelings of inadequacy by overspending on her partner and the home. She may never express her deeper needs and concerns about their relationship. The fear that her husband may leave her or the fact that she needs more physical attention, she keeps secret. By compensating, she is untrue to her real needs and unfair with her husband, who hasn't a clue about what's going on with her.

Identification

Compulsive spenders may identify with a certain person or social group in an obsessive and unrealistic way, becoming so inappropriately focused or identified with the lives of others that they lose sight of their own life issues. One fireman gave ninety percent of his leisure hours to activities related to the firehouse. He became so involved with the fire station that he ignored his serious marital and financial problems.

Atonement

Money abusers practice atonement when they make amends for over-spending on themselves by buying things for someone else. A compulsive spender who purchases a new boat may bring his wife a token gift to atone somehow for his extravagance. Atonement is a short-lived mitigation of the hurt and confusion of others. It involves denial because it diverts attention from the reality of compulsive spending or other money obsessions.

Emotional Isolation and Withdrawal

Money addicts isolate themselves from those who might challenge behavior that has escaped their control. Isolation and withdrawal enable them to live a secret life and deny the problem without inter-ference from others. Ginny, for example, stopped entertaining in her home for fear that creditors would embarrass her in the presence of guests.

Rationalization

Rationalization is a very common coping mechanism among money addicts. A compulsive spender poses seemingly logical justifications of illogical behaviors: "If you had a boss like mine, you'd need to spend now and then to get some relief," or "A cash advance from a new cred-it card will help me meet the minimum payments on my other accounts." Ginny was rationalizing when she continued shopping despite her child's illness, saying that she was thereby avoiding a sec-ond trip.

Alibis

Alibis are stories money addicts tell to prevent confrontation by oth-ers. Ginny told her husband that new clothes were gifts from a friend and new shoes were old.

Euphoric Recall

Spenders subconsciously remember only the good about their spend-ing and forget everything bad. Cindy remembers the pretty outfits she bought and the nice sales clerk, but she does not remember the fight she and her husband had about the expense. Euphoric recall involves denial, screening out an honest picture of behavior.

Minimizing

Money addicts down scale the true seriousness of money abuse. Tom told his wife, "I spent a few bucks at the marine supply store." He actually had spent a few hundred dollars. Minimizing keeps him and others from seeing the reality of his money problems.

Uncovering Denial

How do people know whether they are in denial? Reading this book is a good start. It shows curiosity about spending. Descriptions of compulsive spending styles and phases illuminate facts that denial hides. Sometimes the most courageous and effective way to see whether judgment has been clouded by denial is to ask a caring friend who knows something about the problem. Members of DA, sponsors, therapists, or honest friends or family members are good sources of a fresh viewpoint. They should listen carefully to what is said. Keeping a recovery journal is another way to confront denial and strip it away.

For some, hitting bottom is the only way finally to see the reality of money abuse. Everyone has a different "bottom," and no two people arrive there exactly the same way. Hitting bottom means that there's nowhere to go but up. Sometimes friends and family can intervene to raise someone's bottom through a planned intervention, but usually people reach it in their own way and at their own time. In an era enlightened by accessible information, support systems, and emphasis on recovery, it isn't necessary to take the elevator to the bottom floor; people can get off the anguishing ride at any stop.

Walking through Recovery

It has been said that pain is the great motivator. Having decided to take a honest look at your situation, you will want to know what the journey out of pain and compulsion will be like. Will life improve?

The answer is yes. As your willingness to seek help changes your life, you will see remarkable results. The following ingredients of recovery will help you understand the healing process.

Facing Addiction

Addiction is a foot stomping child inside who says, I want what I want when I want it. It cries out in indignation when needs aren't met. Addiction's only job is to shovel in "pleasures" to fill the empty holes inside. Abuse of money is never enough. The more addiction takes in, the more it demands, and the bigger the hole gets. Pain increases after each attempt to get "enough." Addiction is the endless cycle of trying to satisfy that which cannot be satisfied. The great truth of any addiction is that it never brings satisfaction but only pain and disruption. When people are willing to say *wait* to their addiction, they begin to get well, feeling normal frustrations without running away.

Surrender and Powerlessness

Money addicts proceed in recovery when they admit that they need help. Surrender and the admission that they are powerless over money problems is the bedrock of a recovery program. People who stop fighting and ask for help can listen to others and allow their emotional emptiness to be exposed. That revelation teaches them about their true feelings. They can heal their hurts by using healthy resources instead of medicating them with compulsions.

If you have identified yourself as a money addict and are willing to accept your own powerlessness over money abuse, then it's time for you actually, physically, to do something. Call DA and go to a meeting. Seek help from a consumer credit counseling service. See a therapist. Be honest with the people you've been lying to. As pain teaches, honesty humbles. Surrendering to the seriousness of your money problems brings humility. Letting down defenses to tell others about the pain permits a new sort of vulnerability. One feels sensitive to everything and everyone and doubts that one has the strength to pick up the broken pieces caused by money abuse.

To admit that you have a serious problem is one thing. The leap of faith and belief that you can be helped may seem too high.

Accustomed to pain, you may not know what it's like to feel good or to wake up each morning loving the face you see in the mirror. Self-esteem may be a dim memory that flickers when you try to recapture its light. You may be so full of shame that you can't imagine deserving another chance at a happy life. Recovery challenges you to take leap after leap across open unknown territory. Honest and vulnerable, you are now teachable. Again, you need the courage to learn new ways to stay honest with money. Honesty and courage allow your empty heart to believe that it deserves to be full.

13

Getting Help

Money addiction remains a taboo in our society at a time when other taboos have dissolved. Essential to this addiction is the appearance of having more or less wealth than one actually does, and the effort, by every conceivable machination, to keep the facade from cracking. The high investment in a false image makes it especially difficult for money abusers to seek help. Because so many people successfully project a false image of security and happiness, money addicts often think that they suffer alone. When worry and fear overwhelm them, driving them to confide in friends or family members, sometimes these confidants respond, "Oh, don't worry about it—everybody's in debt!"

Many people avoid talking about money because it's too personal a subject for comfort. Because a person's identity often is linked with spending power, a plea for help reveals buried insecurities and self-doubts. Without help, however, compulsive spending and other money obsessions only give teeth to those doubts and insecurities, enabling them to gnaw away any remaining self-esteem. This chapter suggests several reputable sources that openly face addiction, help to clarify it, and offer supportive directions for recovery.

Debtors Anonymous

When money addicts are tired of the struggle, many organizations can offer them help. DA is one of the most successful. Its program of recovery is based on the Twelve Steps of Alcoholics Anonymous (see the appendix). On the next page are the Steps that members follow in the process of recovery:

In DA, members learn how to stop compulsive money abuse. They have access to a pressure group that can teach them how to relieve pressure by contacting creditors and negotiating a reasonable payment plan, how to establish realistic spending, and how to get out of debt. They also learn in DA about recovery and their right to financial and spiritual prosperity. Developing a capacity for "conscious spending" is one of the program's ultimate goals. DA is free. Members pass a basket to help pay for coffee, rent, and other expenses, but contributions are strictly voluntary.

Some people think it too embarrassing to attend DA. It helps to remember how embarrassing is it to have credit revoked, to lie, hide purchases, or receive creditors' phone calls at work. Becoming involved in a recovery program relieves the shame and embarrassment and helps fill the gap with what was missing all along. It is a comfort that everyone else at the meeting has the same problem.

Sometimes money abusers feel they're too far gone for DA. No matter how much they spend (or fail to spend), however, there always will be a member who has a bigger money problem. Some say they're too busy to go to meetings—can't they just send the info by mail? That's like asking the doctor to deliver a baby via fax. They really *need* to be consistently present at meetings for the program to work. The fellowship of other recovering people is what makes recovery possible. Compulsive money abuse takes a lot of energy; attendance at meetings requires a fraction of that effort.

Poverty addicts may wonder whether DA would welcome them. Yes. Lots of people who are poverty addicts caught in the cycle of deprivation find help at DA. Others who resist the choice to attend DA argue that the Twelve Step programs are all "into religion" and God. All that the organization's principles ask is that members come to believe that a power exists that is greater than themselves. It may be God; the fellowship (surely a whole room full of recovering people is more powerful than one individual); nature— any higher power that they are comfortable with. A deep and comforting spirituality can come to people of all religious backgrounds or none. The spiritual aspect of the Twelve Step Program is open to personal choice. It is an understanding that they are not alone in the world but are carried along and helped by a power greater than themselves that won't abandon them. DA shares the following assessment to help people decide whether they are involved in compulsive debting.

Debtors Anonymous Questionnaire

Most compulsive debtors will answer yes to at least eight of the following fifteen questions:

1. Are your debts making your home life unhappy?
   ☐ Yes   ☐ No
2. Does the pressure of your debts distract you from your daily work?   ☐ Yes   ☐ No
3. Are your debts affecting your reputation?   ☐ Yes   ☐ No
4. Do your debts cause you to think less of yourself?
   ☐ Yes   ☐ No
5. Have you ever given false information in order to obtain credit   ☐ Yes   ☐ No
6. Have you ever made unrealistic promises to your creditors?
   ☐ Yes   ☐ No
7. Does the pressure of your debts make you careless of the welfare of your family?   ☐ Yes   ☐ No
8. Do you ever fear that your employer, family, or friends will learn the extent of your total indebtedness?   ☐ Yes   ☐ No
9. When faced with a difficult financial decision, does the prospect of borrowing give you a feeling of inordinate relief?
   ☐ Yes   ☐ No
10. Does the pressure of your debts cause you to have difficulty in sleeping?   ☐ Yes   ☐ No
11. Has the pressure of your debts ever caused you to consider getting drunk?   ☐ Yes   ☐ No
12. Have you ever borrowed money without giving adequate consideration to the rate of interest you are required to pay?
    ☐ Yes   ☐ No

13. Do you usually expect a negative response when you are subject to a credit investigation?　□ Yes　□ No
14. Have you ever developed a strict regimen for paying off your debts, only to break it under pressure?　□ Yes　□ No
15. Do you justify your debts by telling yourself that you are superior to the "other" people, and when you get your "break" you'll be out of debt overnight?　□ Yes　□ No

The Twelve Steps of Debtors Anonymous

1. We admitted we were powerless over debt—that our lives had become unmanageable.
2. Came to believe that a Power greater than ourselves could restore us to sanity.
3. Made a decision to turn our will and our lives over to the care of God *as we understood God.*
4. Made a searching and fearless moral inventory of ourselves.
5. Admitted to God, to ourselves, and to another human being the exact nature of our wrongs.
6. Were entirely ready to have God remove all these defects of character.
7. Humbly asked God to remove our shortcomings.
8. Made a list of all persons we had harmed and became willing to make amends to them all.
9. Made direct amends to such people wherever possible, except when to do so would injure them or others.
10. Continued to take personal inventory and when we were wrong, promptly admitted it.
11. Sought through prayer and meditation to improve our conscious contact with God *as we understood God,* praying only for knowledge of God's will for us and the power to carry that out.
12. Having had a spiritual awakening as the result of these steps, we tried to carry this message to compulsive debtors, and to practice these principles in all our affairs.

The Twelve Steps of Debtors Anonymous, adapted from the Twelve Steps of Alcoholics Anonymous, with permission.

A number of money related Twelve Step groups are springing up across the country with names like Spenders Anonymous and Shoppers Anonymous; their numbers may be in your local phone book.

To find a local Debtors Anonymous meeting, call information and ask for the local number or call the national hotline in New York at (212) 642-8222. For written information, the address is:

Debtors Anonymous General Service Office
P.O. Box 400
Grand Central Station
New York, NY 10163-0400

Inquiries are confidential. A stamped, self-addressed envelope will bring a faster reply.

Local hospitals and addiction treatment centers are also good sources of information about local support groups and meeting information.

Multiple Addictions

Some people have more than one active addiction. Whichever prob- lem is causing the most pain is generally the one to deal with first. We wholeheartedly recommend that, regardless of which problem takes priority, a Twelve Step group (Alcoholics Anonymous, Narcotics Anonymous, Debtors Anonymous, or another) be tried as part of a recovering person's plans. They complement and reinforce each other and provide a consistent approach that is critical for a sound recov- ery. For years, recovery professionals, believing that people can go only so fast and so far at once, thought that only one addiction should be addressed at a time. At some point in recovery, however, people must address other existing compulsions and excesses. They should not use one recovery program as a way to avoid facing another addiction.

Money problems seem to be the sacred cow of the recovery field. "Talk to me about my other problems, but don't mess with my money" is a statement someone in AA made to a sponsor. The quality of their Twelve Step recovery has been undermined for many members who refuse to be honest about their money games and manipulations. The

AA Program challenges its members to get honest in all areas of their lives in order to live a balanced and serene life.

Finances and Romances

Emil was a recovering alcoholic with eight years of sobriety. He had tried very hard to work his AA program honestly but continued nevertheless to suffer from many highs and lows in his life. His sponsor, Leo, talked with him about being a "dry drunk." Emil hadn't had a drink in eight years, but he still wasn't happy. He reacted defensively at first when Leo said, "You aren't drinking, but your ups and downs in finances and romances are making your life crazy."

Money and relationship problems have been seen as threats to comfortable recovery for many people in Alcoholics Anonymous, Overeaters Anonymous, and other Twelve Step programs. In the last decade, Al-Anon and Adult Children of Alcoholics have addressed relationship issues, but money addiction seldom is acknowledged as a disruption of life balance in recovery. Emil's life began to level out and change significantly when he finally was honest about his "finances and romances."

A comprehensive recovery plan is needed in a situation like Emil's. A therapist who understands addictions can help people to map out a strategy of therapy and Twelve Step work that includes an ongoing review of all life areas. Then recovering money abusers can see how far they have come and in what direction they need to go.

Consumer Credit Counseling

Financial counselors provide education and guidance about money problems but they cannot address the personal issues that contribute to destructive patterns of spending. Be leery of counselors and agencies that charge a fee. With so much free or low-cost help available, it doesn't make much sense to fall deeper into debt while trying to get out of it.

National Foundation for Consumer Credit

NFCC is a nonprofit umbrella group for more than 700 Consumer Credit Counseling Service offices in the United States and Canada. These offices provide free or very inexpensive financial guidance to consumers across the country. The organization's goals are to educate, counsel, and promote the wise use of credit.

To contact a local CCCS office, check the local phone directory under Consumer Credit Counseling Service or call toll free 1-800-388-CCCS (2227). Write to the:

National Foundation for Consumer Credit
8701 Georgia Avenue, Suite 507
Silver Spring, MD 20910

The NFCC's Consumer Credit Counseling Services can help individuals and families contact creditors, establish spending plans, and learn important money management techniques.

How CCCS Works

Anyone overburdened by credit obligations can phone or write or visit a CCCS office. Creditors, clergy, legal aid societies, the Red Cross, and social service or labor representatives also refer clients. The service requires that an application for credit counseling be completed. Applicants arrange an appointment for a personal interview. With broad community backing, a professional counselor prepares a repayment plan acceptable to both client and creditors. Usually the plan is enough unless some emergency or a change in financial situation arises. Further service is available, however, at any time. Counseling usually is free. When the service administers a debt repayment plan, it sometimes charges a nominal fee to defray administrative costs.

Treating the Symptoms

Even the best consumer credit counseling service treats only the symptoms. A usual symptom of compulsive spending is indebtedness.

Consumer Credit Counseling Services focus on this symptom of addiction, not the underlying causes. For a deeper understanding of the dynamics that fuel spending, recovering addicts need to consult a therapist and attend DA meetings.

Finding a Therapist

If you are a compulsive spender or poverty addict, or if you love someone who is, a therapist can help you heal. People who practice self-defeating, self-destructive behaviors need time and assistance to heal the wounds. They didn't occur overnight, and they won't heal overnight. Just as you would consult a surgeon for a damaged heart, so should you consult an expert for a wounded spirit.

Recovery isn't always easy, but it is worth the effort, as Marie found. When she began therapy, she was extremely apprehensive, having had two bad experiences with therapy in the past. Once she had been in marriage counseling with her husband, an alcoholic. The therapist had refused to acknowledge the addiction to alcohol, despite the fact that Marie's husband sometimes came to sessions intoxicated. The therapist knew nothing about the disease of alcoholism. After four years of Al-Anon, Marie can look back now and realize that the therapist simply hadn't been trained adequately. The second time around, Marie consulted her church minister. She left the conference with him feeling even more guilty and responsible than before. Marie hated her first Al-Anon meeting because the members kept the focus on themselves rather than the alcoholic. "I wanted to remain a victim and complain about my rough life," Marie said. "I had cornered the market on suffering, and I wanted the world to know it. For some reason I kept going back to Al-Anon anyway. It has saved my life. Or, rather, it gave me the tools I needed to save myself."

Still Marie felt that some additional work remained. She felt healthier, more confident and sure than ever before. But she had some terrible financial troubles and had switched her problem from her husband to buying. Although she had progressed on one front, on another she was still repeating the same mistakes. Marie had heard that a pattern of making the same mistakes indicates a need for therapy. This time, however, Marie interviewed the therapist, looking for the following qualities:

- **Listening.** It is important when you talk with a therapist that you feel listened to. You may not always agree with or like some of your therapist's interpretations and suggestions, but, if you feel safe and heard, you will be able to trust enough to examine your own reactions and resistances.

- **Validating.** Everyone has good qualities and special gifts. One of the primary goals of your therapy is to help you recognize and accept your own worth. It will be much easier for you to ponder difficulties and problems if you feel that your therapist recognizes and affirms that you are a valuable and unique person. Therapy is not punishment. You have a basic right to feel validated by your therapist.

- **Providing safety.** Your therapy will include the expression of a range of strong feelings as you grieve about your experiences. It is essential that your therapist feel comfortable in encouraging sadness, anger, frustration, and joy. The setting needs to feel safe enough that you can take the lid off your emotions and share your deepest secrets.

- **Setting clear boundaries.** In your initial family, boundaries may have been confused and poorly defined. Therefore it is very important for your therapist to establish clear and appropriate boundaries for your relationship. It will not be appropriate or healing for you to have a friendship or intimate relationship with your therapist outside of therapy.

- **Training and credentials.** You have the right to expect that your therapist has been trained in the field of addiction counseling. The most effective therapists also have received extensive training in the dynamics and process of individual and group therapy.[7]

After reading this book you should have enough information to determine whether a therapist is worth a try. If you decide that a relationship with one therapist isn't going to work, don't go back, but don't give up; see someone else. Just be certain you're not rejecting someone who could help merely because honesty is uncomfortable at first.

You cannot serve your best interest by seeing a therapist who never confronts you.

Marie interviewed three therapists and decided on the third. "I wanted a therapist to help me grow stronger, surer, to accept me and want me to assert myself in order to get my needs met. My therapist did just that and more. The therapist called me on my 'stuff,' didn't let me get away with playing games, but always encouraged me, gently helping me to see."

The best way to find a good therapist is by word of mouth, through friends and relatives and colleagues. If that is not an option, you can call your local social service and mental health agencies for an appropriate referral. DA meetings are a good place to meet people who might be able to recommend a good therapist. Local hospitals and, particularly, addiction treatment centers can suggest names of therapists to whom they refer their patients.

Treatment Centers

Only a few treatment programs are sensitive to compulsive spending and money obsession as a primary addictive process. Some receive insurance reimbursement for their services. You may have to make many phone calls to get one piece of useful information, but don't give up. Think of all the energy you use in worry about money, and know that finding help uses but a fraction of that effort. It will yield a positive outcome.

You Are in a Position of Power

Most creditors would rather deal with you than turn your account over to a collection agency. It usually costs the creditor more money to pay the bill collector than to wait while you pay off the debt by installments.

Bankruptcy

Bankruptcy is not recommended as a part of recovery from compulsive spending. Nor is bankruptcy a component of DA's Twelve Step Program. The most important and basic tools of recovery from money addiction are the spending and debt repayment plans.

If a person works hard at recovery, practices a livable plan to repay debt, and eventually frees himself, he can be proud and satisfied. Chances are he will not repeat the same behavior. If, on the other hand, a judge simply wipes the slate clean and lets him start anew, odds are that the cycle will repeat itself. Quite commonly, people who declare bankruptcy do so again. The procedure treats the symptoms of compulsive debt and spending, not the cause. Bankruptcy opens the way for more symptoms to surface. They inevitably do.

Thus, bankruptcy is just another temporary fix that belongs in the category of cash advances, unsecured loans, and denial. This expedient merely delays confronting the compulsion. In addition, it breeds more of the very feelings of failure and impotence that compel money abusers to overspend and create more debt. For the compulsive spender, bankruptcy is not a constructive option.

Inventory of Daily Spending

Compulsive spenders may leave home in the morning with twenty dollars and return at the end of the day with sixty-three cents, completely unaware of where the money went. They have developed a cavalier attitude about money. They ignore balances, check numbers, and loose change. They neglect to record checks, count change, and look at prices. As their debts mount, they convince themselves that counting pennies is absurd.

Part of recovery is responsibility about the details. Analyzing how that $19.37 was spent helps clarify the choices one makes. It is informative to inventory daily spending for a week or two and then intermittently during recovery.

This inventory is a simple list of all money spent, down to the penny. Yes, it is a pain in the neck to stop several times a day and jot down seventy-five cents for a candy bar or a tablet, but the nuisance pays off. The discipline confirms that you are in control and leaving nothing to chance. It says you claim total responsibility for your spending! A log helps you identify patterns of spending so you can learn to improve your choices.

Some people prefer to plan the day's spending. They take only the cash they need and spend only the amount reserved for that day. Others find that keeping track of the pennies feels healthy and responsible. They enjoy their sense of control.

Abstinence or Plastic Detox

Most professionals in the field of addiction accept the view that abstinence is the only successful treatment for addiction. Alcoholics can't drink, even a little, if they wish to get well. Cocaine addicts can't use coke and nicotine addicts can't have just one puff. So it is with compulsive debtors that abstinence from unsecured credit is the cornerstone of recovery.

You don't abstain for the rest of your life. You abstain for the rest of your life one day at a time. You get through this day only. You don't think about abstaining tomorrow or the next day or the day after that. Abstinence for one day is all that is asked each day. It is possible to do something for twenty-four hours that would be terrifying if we thought we would have to do it forever.

Some people get caught in this trap: Alcoholics can exist without alcohol and ex-smokers can exist without cigarettes, they say, but I still have to earn, spend, and deal with money every day. I can't just give up money! Well, no one need give up money. Abstinence from unsecured debt is all that recovery requires. An unsecured debt is one that is not backed up with collateral. A car loan is secured; the lender can repossess the car if the borrower defaults. A MasterCard, on the other hand, is unsecured.

When someone is concerned about excessive drinking, some people say, "Okay, try limited, controlled drinking. If you can do it, fine—don't go to AA. If you can't, what time shall I pick you up for the meeting?"

You can test yourself similarly with money. If you wish to do so, work with someone from DA, a spending treatment program, a therapist, or someone else who understands this problem and will not make you feel ashamed. Do these things:

- Decide what a healthy, normal use of credit is for you.

- Set up guidelines for conditions under which you will incur debt.

- Decide on an appropriate time limit for the test—thirty days, sixty days, or ninety days.

- If you are able to spend consistently according to your intentions without a lot of anxiety or suffering, you're probably just in the early warning phase. If you cannot consistently spend according to your intentions, for *whatever* reason, it's time to get help and stop the pain, stop the struggle, stop the insanity.

Safe Shopping

People with a compulsion to spend can no more give up money than people with an eating disorder can give up food. It is the *compulsion* that they need to deal with, not the money or the food. When money abusers in initial recovery shop, they benefit from imposing some healthy guidelines on themselves:

- Don't go alone. Take a friend from DA or someone who understands your recovery.

- Whenever possible, call ahead and ask the sales clerk to keep the merchandise you want at the counter for you so you don't find yourself browsing unnecessarily. This plan works well with books, tapes, hardware, and some gift items.

- Make a list and stick to it.

- Bring cash only.

- Decide your needs before you shop. If you want to buy Grandpa a birthday present, plan the purchase (a shirt, a putter, a coffee mug). Avoid the trap of thinking, I'll know it when I see it.

- Don't try to think of some legitimate need just because you're in the mood to shop. That "mood" indicates that something is wrong.

Maybe it's natural emotions you're trying to escape from. If Marie feels anxious because she just lost her job, or if she is hungry or tired or angry, she needs to deal with these normal experiences. Money addicts are not accustomed to experiencing feelings and sensations in a direct way, so at first they may seem raw and over-powering. Learn to embrace your feelings and accept the human condition. The quiet and serenity of noticing what you feel does wonders for self-esteem.

• Call a friend or sponsor before you leave and say what you intend to buy and how much you plan to spend. Afterward, report what happened.

• Enjoy the trip. If you've planned it, told someone about the plan, are not incurring unsecured debts, and are not taking money earmarked for other needs, then enjoy shopping. It's perfectly all right to enjoy buying something new.

• If the craving to spend is fierce, call someone—a friend, sponsor, or fellow DA member.

• Whenever possible, shop at stores that carry only what you need. For example, if you need shoes, go to a shoe store, not a department store.

• Know how you intend to use the item you buy. Do you want shoes to match a lot of different outfits or do you just need some rain boots?

• Don't take any credit cards with you.

• If you abused catalogs or TV shopping, buy only in stores.

• Eat a healthy meal and be well rested. Our defenses are down when we are hungry and tired.

• Examine your mood. Anger or loneliness can weaken the resolve to shop safely.

The three components of recovery are acknowledging the problem, asking for help, and making some of the recommended changes. See a therapist, go to a DA meeting, or visit a Consumer Credit Counseling Service. Andy often told his wife Sherry about his plans for recovery and imagined how wonderful the results would be. Yet he never *acted* to start his recovery. Today, as a recovering money addict, he says, "I used to talk so much about what I planned to do that it felt as if I had actually done it. I really believed that having an idea was the same as following through on the idea with action. I was immobilized by worry." Today Andy has reduced his debt while growing in security, because now he can spend without compulsion. He has replaced his words with action that has brought him prosperity. He found no shame in asking for help, but what a shame it would have been for him to suffer needlessly.

CHAPTER

14

Creating a Recovery Journal

Each compulsive spender needs to be involved actively in her own recovery plan for it to work. It needs to be personal and fit into each person's unique circumstances. While some actions apply to everyone who needs help with compulsive spending, individual differences affect the assimilation of those steps into one's life.

The lack of control is what recovering money addicts need to change. One way to accomplish this goal is to create a spending plan and stick to it. This decision makes life increasingly peaceful. When money addicts learn that happiness comes from within, they possess the power to bring about their own abundance. They control their destiny to a point, but never completely. The goal is to maintain abstinence even when awful things do happen.

A recovery journal is an excellent aid in reclaiming one's destiny. This ongoing diary records personal money issues, goals about money, and continuing progress. A journal is a gift to oneself. It yields more meaningful treasures than all the material possessions in the world. It is not an alternative to DA or therapy. It is a supplement to those sources of help. Because your recovery journal is a gift to yourself, it should be especially attractive. Take great care to select a notebook or diary that you like. Divide it into the following sections:

- Spending Choices
- Creditor Information
- Prosperity Affirmations
- Giving Plan

- Relapse Prevention
- Assets of Recovery

Spending Choices

When Jim hears the word *budget* he conjures up words like *cut, prune, deficit, red, sacrifice, scrimp,* and *slash.* When he hears *spending choices* he thinks of less threatening words like *option, selection, preference,* and *decision.* These are the very words advertisers want people to associate with their credit cards. But for overspenders, credit cards represent restriction. Their use of credit *takes away* their decisions, selections, and options. Budgets feel like punishment, and the last thing most people need is more punishment. Spending choices, however, are a *plan* for expenses. The phrase carries no negative associations.

In order to design your plan, make a list of all current expenses, regardless of whether you can meet those expenses at this time. The following pages present two examples. The first is a plan for Jim and Marcia, a married couple with three children. He is the sole wage earner in the family and makes $96,000 annually. Since the plan affects them both, Jim and Marcia developed it together. The second plan is for Kristin, a single woman of twenty-five. She is an actress making approximately $24,000 yearly.

The following examples and the money management tools outlined in this chapter have come from people who have had continuing success in their recovery from money abuse. These methods are consistent with the philosophy of DA and with the addiction models used so successfully with other compulsive behaviors.

Jim and Marcia's Spending Choices

Monthly Income: $5,800

Categories	Monthly Expenses	New Choices	Actual Expenses
Mortgage	$1,700	$1,700	_____
Utilities	195	195	_____
Transportation	600	500	_____
Clothing	400	200	_____
Food	600	500	_____
Entertainment	400	100	_____
Medical expenses	200	200	_____
Recreation	150	0	_____
Personal expenses	200	100	_____
Periodicals and newspapers	40	20	_____
Education	282	282	_____
Bank card	300	275	_____
Bank card	200	200	_____
Bank card	350	350	_____
Department store card	186	150	_____
Department store card	195	150	_____
Department store card	307	307	_____
Department store card	402	350	_____
Gas card	36	36	_____
Gas card	30	30	_____
Personal loan	350	200	_____

Total current expenses:	$7,123	
Total new choices	$5,845	
Total actual income:	$5,800	Monthly income
	-5.845	New choices
	$ -45	

When a child cries out in the night, afraid of what creatures might be lurking about his room, a sensitive parent turns on the light so the child can see for himself that he's safe. We adults are afraid as well of things we cannot see. A spending choices plan turns on the light and reveals the resources for bringing order to financial chaos.

There are two obvious ways to balance the books, eliminating the discrepancy between expenses and income: (1) reduce expenses, and (2) add more income. Most people find it helpful or necessary to do both.

Ways to Reduce Expenses

In the second column of their spending choices plan Jim and Marcia made some new choices about how they wanted to spend their money.

• They reduced transportation expenses by one hundred dollars. Jim decided that he no longer would park in expensive garages. Though he would have to walk farther when he parked in lots, the additional exercise would benefit his health.

• Jim needed a classic, conservative wardrobe for his profession. The children were continually outgrowing shoes, coats, boots, and other items of clothing. Jim and Marcia decided that they realistically could reduce their monthly clothing expense by $200. Some of the children's clothing could be mended instead of discarded and many items could be purchased at resale shops and garage sales. In addition, Jim could launder and iron his five dress shirts weekly instead of taking them to the cleaners. These three adjustments saved $200 in the clothing category.

• Jim and Marcia agreed to shop at a less expensive supermarket. It meant a little inconvenience, since they had to bag their own groceries at the new store, but they saved money on food. Marcia also used discount coupons and rebates.

• Jim and Marcia agreed to replace elegant dinners out with carryout pizza and rental videos. It was just as much fun (and less stressful) to invite another couple over for dessert and Trivial Pursuit as it was to host a complicated dinner party. They practically eliminated fast-food lunches for themselves and the kids. Fast food was not only an unnecessary expense but also provided poor nutrition.

Jim and Marcia were treating themselves better, and it began to feel good.

• They canceled their memberships at health clubs. This change was the most difficult. They both relied heavily on their exercise regimens to control weight and work off stress. They changed their exercise habits to include walking, swimming at the local high school, and playing tennis at free outdoor courts and basketball at the neighborhood park.

• Personal expenses were curtailed. Marcia cut the girls' hair herself instead of taking them to beauty shops. Jim began to shine his own shoes. Marcia switched from department store cosmetics to drug-store brands.

• Marcia and Jim agreed that they wasted money by subscribing to more magazines than they had time to read. They reduced that expense by half.

• Jim and Marcia contacted creditors and asked for reduced monthly payments. Some creditors were cooperative and others not.

• The couple renegotiated a loan they had from Jim's brother.

After reducing expenses Jim and Marcia were still forty-five dollars shy of meeting their expenses (see the end of their spending choices plan). Since they already had reduced expenses as much as they thought possible, they planned to increase their income to cover the forty-five dollar discrepancy that remained.

Jim used a page in his journal to list every conceivable way to create more income. He left plenty of space to add ideas later. His list looked like this:

Ways to Add Income

1. Sell coin collection.
2. Hold garage sale.
3. Sell old clothes on consignment.
4. Look for loose change in old coat pockets, drawers, glove compartments, and chairs.
5. Cash in jar of pennies that has been filling up on dresser since 1981.

6. Rent out extra room, garage, or storage space.
7. Collect debts owed to me.
8. Marcia take on part-time job.
9. Marcia baby-sit at home.
10.
11.

Jim and Marcia reviewed the list of ways to add income and chose to hold a garage sale, sell the coin collection, and turn in change at the bank. Marcia decided to do a little baby-sitting at home as well.

These income sources yielded an immediate total of $1,200 cash and another $120 monthly income from the baby-sitting. Jim and Marcia used the $1,200 cash to pay off both gas credit cards and buy some child safety gates and miscellaneous supplies needed for Marcia's baby-sitting. The baby-sitting income and the elimination of payments on the gas credit cards brought the family to $141 above their monthly expenses.

Jim and Marcia then completed the third column of figures, "Actual Expenses." There they recorded whether their actions matched their intentions. Unlike budgets, spending choices plans are flexible, and they evolve over time. Sometimes a new choice doesn't work out as planned. Sometimes a forgotten expense must be added, or an unexpected medical or dental expense arises. In this case, an additional $141 a month was acquired and decisions had to be made about how to spend this money. As recovering overspenders decrease debt and start thinking and acting in ways that make more money available, they add new categories to their plans. Vacations and home improvement are common additions.

The reason for recovering from compulsive spending and debting is to bring abundance and prosperity into your life. As you begin creating strategies for recovery, define what those words, *prosperity* and *abundance*, mean to you. You can use our definitions or write your own. As we see it, prosperity is a condition of thriving and growing with a focus on improving the quality of one's financial and emotional life. Abundance is a feeling and attitude of plenty in life with ample monetary and emotional wealth.

Pay Yourself First

If you remove all pleasure from your life and live just to pay debt, you won't last very long. In your spending choices plan you must set aside money for things that make you happy. You need to fulfill your obligations to creditors, but you should not destroy the quality of your life. Of course, if you have a pattern of gross overindulging in a particular area, you need to significantly reduce that category, but you never should eliminate it.

You pay yourself for necessities and for pleasure. You pay yourself for shelter, food, clothing, and medical attention because you need these things to survive. You also pay yourself for pleasures because recovery is not about deprivation, it is about abundance.

If an accountant were to analyze Jim and Marcia's spending choices plan, she might find ways to reduce expenses even further. And she would be right—some of the time. If someone is not addicted and is merely in a temporary financial jam, bare-bones living might be the way to approach the problem. Several months or a year or two of scrimping and sacrificing would be tolerable and a successful solution. For addicted people, however, this strategy not only would fail, it also could exacerbate the problem.

For people who spend in order to soothe their pain and care for themselves in the best and only way they know how, a life of extreme deprivation would likely re-create the same feelings that fostered the addiction in the first place. If Jim and Marcia cut their food bill further, requiring her to bake her own bread and can her own home-grown foods while taking care of additional children and giving up all other extras, and if Jim took on a weekend job, spending less time with his family and pitching in around the house, the changes would cause more anxiety and frantic living. Recovery requires serenity and time for clear and thoughtful reflection. Recovery necessitates that you take time to enjoy and experience the people you love. You need the peace and quiet to feel your feelings and not sprint in the other direction when feelings present themselves. Going to the other extreme by removing all of the flavor in life and scheduling more chaos surely will backfire.

While figures don't lie, and math is an exact science, our emotions are anything but precise. When the financial data of a money addict are considered, both the numbers and the emotional needs must be weighed to strike a healthy balance. This fact does not imply that money addicts should not face the consequences of their behavior or should be treated with kid gloves. It simply means that addiction is two sided, one side representing the dollars and cents and the other the emotions. Jim and Marcia are working to repay debt; they are taking full ownership and responsibility for their actions. In doing so they must retain some of what makes life a pleasure rather than a sentence. Adding color to our existence makes us want to go on and keep trying.

Not all of life's pleasures cost money. When devising a spending plan try not to overlook the simple enjoyments that are free or close to it. Make a list and draw from it when planning how to spend your money.

Free (or Almost Free) Pleasures

1. Back rubs and massages.
2. Games—board games, card games, word games, scavenger hunts, and other "action" games.
3. Walks on the beach, in the woods, on nature trails.
4. Architectural tours by bus.
5. The public library and museums.
6. Reading.
7. Experimental cooking.
8. Long talks over coffee or tea.
9. Free community- or university-sponsored concerts.
10. Readings and lectures.

Money addicts must include pleasures in their lives whether they're free, low cost, or simply an allowed expense. Knowing how much to cut, how much to spend, and how much to pay may be difficult, but that's why DA and other help sources exist. No one has to make the trip to financial and emotional health alone. And no one should.

Kristin's Spending Choices

Monthly Income Approximately: $1,825

Categories	Monthly Expenses	New Choices	Actual Expenses
Rent (includes utilities)	$500	$250	_____
Clothing	200	150	_____
Transportation	200	200	_____
Food	400	400	_____
Medical expenses	40	40	_____
Business expenses	25	25	_____
Union dues	50	50	_____
Phone	50	50	_____
Personal expenses	100	50	_____
Entertainment	200	100	_____
Education	70	70	_____
Dry cleaning and laundry	25	25	_____
Bank card	175	90	_____
Bank card	160	80	_____
Department store card	163	80	_____
Department store card	125	90	_____
Department store card	151	70	_____

Total current expenses:	$2,634	
Total new choices:	$1,820	
Total actual income:	$1,825	Monthly income
	-1,820	New choices
	$ 5	

Kristin realized that her monthly expenses significantly exceeded her income. Since she was a freelance actress, she earned no money in some months and several thousand dollars in others. Kristin remembered only the "good" months. She based her lifestyle on her earnings during the few good months of the year instead of taking into account the overall financial picture. This problem is common for people with fluctuating incomes. Believing that they will make large amounts of money in the future, they spend today, confident that their ship will come in and rescue them tomorrow.

Though it was painful, Kristin faced reality. With the help and guidance of other recovering spenders, she was able to get a clear picture of what she spent and what types of denial she used to justify it. Her spending choices plan helped her toward financial solvency and personal growth. Like Jim and Marcia, Kristin made her lists of ways to reduce expenses and ways to increase income:

Ways to Reduce Expenses

1. Get a roommate.
2. Buy fewer clothes:
   - Borrow clothes from another actress instead of buying them when an audition or role calls for something special.
   - Shop the resale stores.
   - Wear existing clothes longer before replacing them.
3. Reduce personal expenses by going to a less expensive salon. Give cards instead of gifts. Buy less expensive cosmetics.
4. Reduce entertainment costs:
   - Take advantage of free or low cost entertainment: out door concerts, parks and beaches, hiking, picnics instead of restaurant lunches, museums, and free lectures and exhibits.
   - Rent videos instead of going to a movie.
   - Allow a friend to pick up tab rather than pay own way to prove independence.
5. If necessary, contact creditors and try to work out a livable repayment plan.

Ways to Increase Income

1. Get a part-time job.
2. Sell diamond ring.
3. Sell antique chair.
4. Sell violin.
5. Ask parents for money.
6.

For Kristin, the hardest thing was the decision to forgo asking her parents for money. She knew that doing so would be a step backward instead of forward. She would be looking for a quick fix instead of an honest solution.

In addition to reducing expenses, Kristin added income by getting an evening job as a waitress ($425 monthly salary), finding a roommate ($250 additional monthly income), and selling her ring ($500 cash). Since she was already two months behind on the rent, she paid the $500 to the landlord.

After Kristin reduced expenses and added income, she was five dollars above her monthly expenses. However, if her income dropped, a real possibility, she would have to reconsider her spending choices further. The only thing left to do was to contact her creditors and to try to work out a lower monthly payment plan.

Because of her payment history, some of the creditors were not amenable to her request for reduced payments. However, Kristin sent what she had told them she would be able to pay each month. She followed up each installment with a letter outlining her repayment plan. She received angry letters and was told to return her cutup cards, which she gladly did. All but one creditor finally accepted that she was doing all she could do. When he took her to court, Kristin worked to avoid resentment, realizing that her creditors did have a right to their money and that her financial problems were not their fault. She took her written financial data to court and showed that she was honestly trying to pay her debts to the best of her ability. The judge ruled that the creditor had to accept her payment plan.

A spending choices plan should include the following elements (see "Spending Choices Plan Worksheet" in appendix):

1. A complete list of all monthly expenses. Convert weekly, annual, or semiannual expenses to a monthly amount. Total these expenses, and deduct them from your total monthly income. Record the resulting figure, even if it is negative.
2. A list of all possible ways to add income, no matter how little money each would bring.
3. A list of all possible ways to reduce expenses. Enter these reductions in the third column of the spending choices list.

4. A "special circumstances" plan. Because of the possibility of prolonged unemployment, Kristin needed a plan for such emergencies. Otherwise she might have been forced to make one later at a time when she could not think as clearly.

One of the most significant ways to reduce expenses is to pay off or begin to make a dent in high interest loans and credit balances. Interest is money you pay that brings you absolutely nothing in return except more and longer payments. Often, paying the minimum or below minimum payment on a credit balance amounts to paying nothing on the principle and everything toward the interest. For this reason, consideration should be given to paying as much as possible toward these debts. High-interest debts should be given highest priority in the spending choices plan.

Expense Categories

Mortgage	Mortgage loan, real estate taxes, and homeowners insurance.
Rent	Rent for place of residence as well as for storage space or garage space.
Utilities	Gas, electricity, water, phone, and garbage pickup.
Transportation	Auto loan, auto insurance, car phone, fuel, car washes, parking, tolls, parking tickets, and public transportation.
Clothing	All clothing, boots, shoes, pantyhose, coats, gloves, and accessories.
Food	Groceries and other items purchased at the supermarket, such as paper and personal care products.
Education	Student loans, seminars, college classes, children's preschool, and any other educational endeavor costing money.
Entertainment	Restaurants, movies, theater, vacations, video

	rentals, spectator sporting events, and anything else one buys or does for enjoyment that costs money, including records, books, tapes, and liquor.
Insurance	Medical, dental, and renter's insurance. Also insurance on special items or valuables.
Medical costs	Prescriptions, glasses, contacts, dentistry, and all other expenses not covered by insurance.
Union dues	All costs pertaining to union membership or membership in professional organizations.
Recreation	All expenses related to hobbies, sports, or athletics, such as health club or country club memberships, golf, bowling, hunting, ceramics classes, sailing lessons, boats, snowmobiles, musical instruments, and knitting yarn.
Household	Furnace repair, new stereo, the chimney sweep, paint, wallpaper, furniture, lawn mower, and all other expenses related to the house or apartment.
Pets	Shots and other veterinarian costs, licenses, tags, boarding, and any other expenses related to pets.
Personal	Includes cosmetics, beauty salon or barber, manicures and pedicures, massages, jewelry, gifts, and greeting cards.
Laundry	Dry-cleaning services and any other outside cleaning, pressing, and mending of clothes.
Periodicals and newspapers	Any publication by subscription.
Bank credit cards	MasterCard, Visa, Discover, and others.
Department store credit cards	Bloomingdale's, J.C. Penney, and others.
Personal loans	Loans with family or friends.
Income tax	Outstanding debt to state or federal tax bill.

Creditor Information

The creditor information section of the journal should contain the names of creditors and lenders, the names of contact people, a record of all telephone and written correspondence, and payment records what you owe, what you have paid, the interest rate, and an updated balance. Here are a couple of samples.

First Bank VISA

Contact person:	Mary Smith
Address:	1 First Bank Plaza
	Anytown, USA
Phone:	(000) 111-0000, extension 304

Agreed monthly payment:	$250.00
Balance:	$13,504.63
Interest rate:	20 percent

Date Paid	Amount	Check Number	Balance
11/1/91	$250.00	304	$13,479.63
12/1/91	$250.00	328	$13,453.63

Mom

Address:	307 Elm Street
	Hometown, USA
Phone:	(222) 222-2222

Agreed monthly payment:	$6.00
Balance:	$3,000.00
Interest rate:	0 percent

Date Paid	Amount	Check Number	Balance
11/1/91	$6.00	309	$2,994.00
12/1/91	$6.00	340	$2,988.00

The monthly payment may not always be easy to agree on. Despite a healthy spending choices plan, there still may not be enough money to pay what the creditor wants.

15

Going Forward in Recovery

With the recovery journal and the spending choices plan, the money addict has established a system for keeping records and has organized present spending in a thoughtful way. These strategies are practical actions to restore order to one's life. In its underlying intentions, however, the program recommended here differs from ordinary budgeting. The problems identified as money misuse and obsession are not moral failures but adaptations, means that people evolve to soothe anxiety and other emotional pain. As in other addictions, the more anguish money misuse causes, the more the addict misuses money to relieve that anguish. Addicts use money as a green over-the-counter drug.

Debt is not only a practical problem, then, but a symptom of deeper needs. Money loses its power to control people's lives as they become aware of their real emotional needs and gradually develop skills for meeting them in a more direct way. This program relieves the anxiety that has increased the reliance on the money drug; at the same time, it helps to mold attitudes about money into a new shape that can be a true guide and comfort in the years ahead. People needn't do everything at once; one logical change at a time is the way out of the overwhelming confusion. The next move forward is a plan to pay off debt.

Calling Your Creditors

Karen was $106,000 in debt. Even after reducing expenses as much as she could, her income could barely cover the minimum amount due on her credit cards. So she mustered all of her assertiveness and, after practicing with her therapist, made phone calls. She called every credit card company she owed, twenty-six in all, and asked for a reduction in minimum payments. She explained that she was in a debt recovery program and wished to pay regularly until the debt was discharged. Explaining that she had drawn up a spending choices plan, she told her creditors what monthly payments she could make. Some of the companies were not happy with the arrangement but nevertheless agreed. Others were less cooperative. Karen had to tell them that they could expect her checks anyway. Often the first person who took her call had no authority to approve the reduced payments, so she had to ask to talk to someone in a higher position. Even those companies that initially refused to negotiate with her became more agreeable when Karen was true to her word and sent the money like clockwork, just as she had promised.

At first Karen sent a short confirmation note to her contact person at the time of each payment (see facing page).

During the first few months, she phoned her contact person in addition to sending a note. Phone calls such as these are not easy, but people make them for several reasons:

- They usually work. When a person is direct and does not promise what she cannot deliver, most creditors accept some payment rather than none, albeit grudgingly.

- Making phone calls is a good way to own the consequences of addictive spending.

- The discipline takes the monster into the light, where one can see that most of the fear was unfounded. When a person stops shoving bills into drawers or bags or purses or garbage cans and starts (however slowly) to confront them, they lose their threat.

- Personal contact with creditors shows good faith. They see that the debtor is trying to meet obligations, not hide from them.

November 1, 19__

Sara Richards
First Bank Credit
000 First Bank Street
Anytown, USA
Re: Acct. no. 7336-0909-339

Dear Ms. Richards:

As I explained on the phone today, I am in a debt recovery program. I will be able to send twenty dollars per month to be applied toward my balance of $604 until the debt is paid. I will mail my monthly payment on the first day of each month beginning now. If at some point I am able to send more, I will. Thank you for your cooperation as I work toward retiring my debts.

Sincerely,

Karen Smith

Here are some guidelines for telephone calls to creditors:

• If you have twenty-six phone calls to make, do not make them all at once. Plan an agenda and stick to it. For instance, you could call four creditors a day until you have contacted them all.

• Ask a sponsor from DA or a friend whom you trust to stay with you while you telephone.

• If no one is available to be with you, arrange to call a friend and report how the phone calls went when you are through.

• Don't promise to send more money than you are able to pay. Dishonesty would make matters worse later.

• Be prepared for difficult conversations. Role-play with a therapist or someone from DA to prepare for the stress.

Creditors may ask you to cut up your credit cards and send them back. That's a very good idea. If a company turns your account over to a collection agency, cooperate. Your recovery depends on the process of paying off your debt in a planned, systematic fashion, facing your own responsibility in your predicament.

No matter what your creditors do, your phone calls to them are important. Businesses don't want to use collection agencies because they often cannot charge as high an interest rate as the credit card issuer. The agency generally keeps a percentage of collections, so your credit card issuer stands to make more money by accepting your payment over time. The phone calls also contribute to your emotional recovery, teaching you to deal straightforwardly with problems and to confront shame. Doing so, you are taking control of your life, which reinforces your sense of personal power.

Moratoriums on Bank Loans and Restructuring

It is best to talk face to face when you are negotiating special financial arrangements. A lender respects a personal visit more than a phone call. The chances of renegotiating a loan are better when you call for an appointment and bring in your written financial data to discuss with the loan officer. Sometimes a moratorium on loans and mortgages can be arranged. This agreement between lender and borrower temporarily interrupts payments or sometimes requires only payment of interest for a period of one to several months. Rather than accept late or erratic payments, a lender occasionally benefits by allowing a few months' respite while the borrower gets back on track.

Personal Loans

Personal loans from friends and family should, if possible, be renegotiated in person. These lenders may feel betrayed and angry if you fail to pay what you owe them, but they may be open to compromise when you face them and take responsibility. Again, it helps to explain that you are in recovery from compulsive spending and to listen to their thoughts and feelings about your poor repayment record. Others have as much right to tell you how they feel as you do to tell them about your recovery and your need for restructuring.

Methods of Payment

Some overspenders are unable to use checks. If you have a history of writing bad checks or if playing games with your checkbook is part of your addiction, then you should hold yourself to a cash-only policy. Banks make this choice for some people. Many compulsive spenders are refused checking accounts by banks because of a lengthy history of bounced checks. This policy works to the spender's advantage. The checkbook is dangerous in the hands of some compulsive spenders. It could only lead to more debt, more misery. A money abuser can manage his affairs very well without ever writing a check. Harold's story, like the stories of many others, confirms this fact.

Harold is a sales representative who, with the help of his employer, found DA. His credit card bills were always in arrears, and he had been arrested for writing bad checks. Early in recovery, Harold had plenty of excuses to defend his desire for a checking account:

"I don't have time to run around getting money orders and cashier's checks to pay my bills every month."

"I can't carry that much cash on me; I might get mugged or lose it."

"Traveler's checks and money orders cost money. I can't afford them."

"People will think something is wrong f I don't have a checking account."

Harold was still nursing a mentality of deprivation. He focused on the effort involved in getting cashier's checks, money orders, and traveler's checks and the hassle of doing business without a checkbook. He allowed self-pity to mask his problem with checks and money.

Changing an attitude of deprivation to one of gratitude takes time. Recovering overspenders have leaned on their compulsion for so long that abstinence may be difficult. For that reason, recovery groups are helpful. His acquaintance with others in DA who got along well without a checkbook showed Harold that his fears were groundless. Most people in recovery who abstain from writing checks feel pride and gratitude with every cashier's check they use. Harold is living proof to newcomers in DA that even business people can live without a checkbook.

Abstinence from Unsecured Credit

Individuals who continue to incur debt despite destructive consequences need abstinence as the cornerstone of their recovery. Refraining from unsecured credit means borrowing only with collateral. A home mortgage is a secured loan because the lender can keep the house if the borrower defaults on the loan. A VISA card debt is not a secured loan because no collateral backs it up.

Joan *needed* minor surgery on her foot. She did not have medical insurance or any extra money in her spending plan, and the operation would cost $1,400. Her friend Nina offered to lend her the money. Joan was determined not to incur debt, however; she believed in her recovery. Her surprising attitude of calm confidence instead of panic pleased her. She met Nina with her recovery journal in hand. She also brought her gold bracelet that Nina had admired.

Joan said that she wanted to accept Nina's offer of a loan, but she insisted on presenting her bracelet as collateral. Initially Nina felt hurt. She trusted Joan; the offer of collateral spoiled the enjoyment of helping a friend. After much discussion, Joan asked, "If I were an alcoholic, would you try to talk me into having a drink?" She explained that an unsecured loan is as dangerous to a money abuser as drugs are to an addict.

Joan was able to receive the medical attention she needed, while Nina knew Joan more intimately. They shared something, a part of Joan's recovery. Joan did pay Nina back, slowly, as scheduled. By setting small payments she did not set herself up to fail. She planned to succeed, and she did.

Addiction is a tricky enemy. Its sleight-of-hand logic lures addicts back to compulsive behavior. False beliefs held in our culture about credit and its importance make the adversary even more difficult to contend with.

A variety of assumptions impede money abusers' recovery:

I cannot rent a car without a credit card. Yes, you can. Most rental car companies permit this practice. Call first to learn the details.

I am in business. When I travel I need a credit card to rent a hotel room. No, you do not. Hotels accept advance deposits by check. Call first for details.

I need my credit cards for emergencies. Exactly what kinds of emergencies? If you trust your spending plans completely, eventually you will know that you have the means to be secure even in a crisis. You are capable of handling whatever comes your way without credit cards. Clever ads and public relations ploys cannot be allowed to undermine your confidence in your ability to take care of yourself.

Some people have found that a debit card fills their need for identification, while at other times a credit card is expected. A debit card resembles a credit card but acts like a check. The bank immediately deducts the price of a purchase from the account and charges no interest. There may be a nominal fee for the card, but it is not debt or interest. If you have a history of misusing checks, however, a debit card is not recommended.

But what about my credit rating? I have to charge things and pay my bills in order to achieve a good credit rating. Why? To get more credit? A credit rating merely qualifies a person for credit. Anyone who abstains from measured credit does not need more.

But what about buying a house or a car? You sure need a good credit rating to borrow for those. You can get around this seeming obstacle. Digging will be necessary, but some lawyers specialize in helping people find lenders who will work with you. DA members and consumer credit counselors also can give you good information and assistance. The point is this: If compulsive spending is ruining your life, then it is time to stop destroying yourself. At the point of financial and emotional ruin, you already have tried all sorts of plans, budgets, promises, and pacts. Now is time to try what works—abstinence.

Prosperity Affirmations

Affirmations are powerful forms of prayer that affirm with expectancy the blessings and riches we would like to have in our lives. Written or repeated regularly, affirmations allow an attitude that anticipates prosperity rather than scarcity. Money addicts who use affirmations in their recovery are amazed at the quick and positive results. Some people talk directly to God or another higher power about the good things they want in life.

Sam is one person who benefits from affirmations. When he joined DA, he learned to trust himself and others. He mourned the losses in his life and found healthy ways to fill the emptiness he always had felt. Now when he becomes fixated on thoughts like, I will never get out of debt, he turns to his wife, his friends, his sponsor, and his personal affirmations to meet his real emotional needs. He uses affirmations and his developing attitude about prosperity to quell his fear of abandonment, deprivation, and loss.

Here are some affirmations to help you develop your own attitudes. Say and write each statement you choose twenty-five times every day. You can select the ones most meaningful to you and gradually add to the list until you have your own personal set of affirmations. Always state them in the present tense.

- I completely and lovingly forgive myself for all of the unhealthy money choices I have made. Today I have grace and wisdom, and I am making healthy money choices.

- I have overflowing abundance in my life today. Healthy ideas for prosperity come to me at the right and perfect time. I act on these ideas with confidence and assurance.

- Today I trust my ability to meet all of my money needs. I completely let go of my fears.

- To me, abundance means having more than enough support and fellowship.

- I am meeting my basic needs as I pay myself first. Now I have the strength to pay all of my obligations.

- Today I am not incurring one more dollar of unsecured debt.

- Abundance fills my life.

- Yesterday is gone. I don't know about tomorrow, but today I am perfectly safe and protected.

- It's okay to succeed.

- I handle money well.

- It's okay to want more money.

- I feel attractive no matter what I wear.

- It's okay to want nice things.

- I can give freely to myself and others.

- I can receive freely with gratitude.

Giving Plan

The giving plan section of a journal is just as important as the spending choices. It is a way to balance your life. Those who have a problem with compulsive spending are so used to the extreme mood swings that accompany the condition that the idea of feeling balanced seems too good to be true. It *is* true and possible, and one of the ways to achieve it is through giving.

Two kinds of attitudes toward giving prevail among compulsive spenders. Some believe they haven't really given unless it was a major sacrifice for them. They give so much that they often feel exhausted and unappreciated. Others don't do much giving because they don't know how, they believe they can't afford it, or they are waiting until they come into great wealth and can write huge checks. These people are not selfish. They simply don't know the value of what they have to offer. They don't believe that what they are now is valuable enough to share.

It is essential to your recovery that you give to others and that you have a plan for doing so. Contributing one dollar a week to your favorite charity may seem cheap, but if it's all you can afford, it is very generous. Below are some ways others have chosen to give.

- Bake one food item a week (or month) and take it to a soup kitchen.
- Spend one afternoon each week as a Big Brother or Big Sister.
- Send a check or money order to a favorite charity once a month.
- Enter a walk-a-thon to raise money for charity.
- Volunteer a few hours a month for the Special Olympics.
- Shovel someone's driveway.
- Mow the lawn for an ill or elderly person.
- Involve yourself in a local community government and work for positive change.
- Visit a nursing home weekly to talk with residents who don't receive many guests.
- Send letters and baked goods to overseas military people.
- Collect items from closets, attics, and basements to donate to charity.
- Spend a few hours each month at a hospital, holding an addicted infant.

People can devise limitless alternative ways to be generous with others. Check newspapers, libraries, and the phone book for reputable charities and helping organizations. Whatever you do, be consistent and follow through. If you wait, the "right time" never will come. You need a plan that includes details for implementation.

Phil left such details out of his plan. He volunteered for the Special Olympics and wanted to teach disabled children to enjoy baseball. His plan didn't work, though, because it didn't specify *when* he would make the inquiries about involvement in the Special Olympics. He didn't decide *how often* he would participate. He neglected to *set a time limit* for obtaining the information. Although he wrote down his intentions in his journal, he did not include the particulars: how, where, when, with whom, the cost (if any), goals, and alternate plans.

Giving can work in reverse, too. Giving compulsively won't absolve the guilt of compulsive spending. Jennifer volunteered at Meals On Wheels and the Special Olympics and also planned to tutor disadvantaged youths. The more time Jenny spent away from home with these activities, the less time she had with her own children and husband. She was filled with guilt about everything, even matters beyond her control. What she finally accepted was that overgiving wouldn't remove her guilt; in fact, it created more. She discovered that the only way to exorcise her guilt was to forgive herself completely and lovingly. She forgave her spending and debts, her attractiveness, and her having healthy children and a nice home. She forgave past mistakes and the pain she had caused herself and others. To the people she had hurt, she made amends. Slowly she let go of the guilt that was crippling her. Jenny was one of those generous people who, if they don't scale down their ambitions, tend to self-destruct in the name of charity. Once she began to value herself without guilt, she found a healthy balance between giving to herself and to others.

Generosity teaches people that they are valuable enough to share. It helps them focus on things other than themselves. Giving, they also receive.

Anonymous gifts assure that one truly gives with no strings. No one knows, so no one congratulates the giver or tells others about the divine act of generosity. The benefactor gives purely, without a thought for self-gain—the essence of charity.

Relapse Prevention

Recovery necessitates knowledge of warning triggers for relapse. Often early recovery is the most difficult period, a time when an addict is especially prone to relapse into old behavior. Many money abusers report the following warning triggers:

- Stores, malls, catalogs, and home shopping shows
- Certain friends
- Restaurants

- Traveling
- Being alone
- Conflict with spouse
- A call or late notice from creditors
- A weight gain
- A disappointment such as a canceled date
- Career or job stress
- The death of a friend or loved one
- A family get-together
- Working long hours
- Complaining about money
- Increased isolation
- Frantic thinking
- Not including time in your schedule for meditation or reflection
- Skipping an appointment with your therapist or missing DA meetings
- Poor record keeping in the checkbook
- Playing with money (buying lottery tickets, playing bingo)
- Extreme anger about the cost of goods
- Extreme anger at the spending habits of others
- Clouding, detaching from behavior as if someone else were committing your actions
- Excesses such as watching too much TV, drinking alcohol, day dreaming, overeating, or undereating

These are just examples. Everyone has powerful individual relapse warning triggers. Record yours in your journal to sharpen awareness. Preparation improves control.

In a trigger situation when you feel the urge to spend in inappropriate ways, change the way you think about your pain or discomfort.

When Larry perceives a snub, he always has a strong urge to spend. Larry recorded this trigger in his journal along with his decision to call his DA sponsor in such a situation. Larry's acceptance and toleration of his feelings led to an understanding that he had allowed others to control his moods and actions, and he decided to take back the control.

Record warning trigger situations in your journal. Then record a plan of action for each. Here's an example:

Trigger	Plan
Shopping for Christmas presents	I will list exactly what to buy and how much to spend. I'll share the plan with someone I trust before I go and again when I return.
Talking to my father. I always feel like spending afterward.	I won't talk to my father until I have had at least four weeks of recovery. I will also call Andy before and after the call.

By preparing yourself, you significantly reduce the chances of relapse. Writing a plan to deal with anticipated problems is an effective way to be prepared. If you do return to old money abuse behavior, it is essential to forgive yourself immediately and realize that difficulty is part of the learning process.

Assets of Recovery

This section of your journal lists the benefits of your recovery. Sometimes overspenders relapse because they become complacent. A list of the gifts you have received from recovery reminds you of progress and illuminates the contrast between your old and new lives. The following is an example:

My recovery has given me

- A renewed and growing trust in my ability to make money and take care of myself.

- Emotional security. I have found internal peace where once there was chaos and turmoil.
- Freedom from financial worries. I no longer spend my days worrying about money and living in fear.
- The ability to plan my spending free of guilt. I have more money to spend than before.
- New friends who accept me as I am.
- Pride. I've paid two bills in full.
- Freedom from shame and guilt. These feelings are beginning to leave me.
- Courage. I try new things that challenge me. I feel comfortable setting high goals for myself. I think about abundance in my life instead of lack.
- Peace with my past. I'm learning to accept my past and not let it ruin the present.
- A new love of myself.
- A new ability to handle money well.
- A knowledge that I have everything I need today.

Some people like to note the date they added each new gift of recovery. The list grows steadily, for recovery brings more joy than any purchase ever did. Reinforce the changes in your life with awareness of the good results.

Your recovery journal is a map. It points you in the right direction, tells you if you're headed off course, and shows you how far you've come and where you still need to go. Your old behavior had you going in circles. Now you can chart your own destinations.

This chapter is a general overview. It does not represent all circumstances and individual differences. It is simply a guide through the fundamentals of early recovery. Doubtless some people will read the suggestions, muttering, "Yeah, but what about. . . ." The yeah buts are genuine concerns. This book cannot possibly address every situation. That is another reason why attending Debtors Anonymous and investigating other help sources are so important.

CHAPTER

16

The Eight Freedoms

Recovery from compulsive spending, credit abuse, and money manipulation brings self-knowledge. When you can look at yourself in the
mirror without flinching, you will enjoy new freedom. With the growth
of honesty, fear of other people, places, and events diminishes. Recovery
provides the tools for a life grounded in harmony and balance. With
increasing health comes acute awareness of the constrictions that once
bound the money-obsessed person. Every move toward recovery weak-
ens the bonds and enlarges freedom.

Freedom from Fear of Exposure

Caught in the grip of compulsive spending, money addicts became
fugitives, their basic sense of security and safety demolished. Expecting
the worst, they open their eyes in dread each morning. In recovery,
you no longer fear being caught. There is nothing to hide. A sane
spending plan and honesty with yourself and others allows you to look
the world in the face. You can answer the phone and the door and
open your mail with ease. No surprises will spring out to get you. You
fall asleep without chronic anxiety and fear.

Freedom from Frantic Planning

Scheming became the focus of the money addicts' every waking minute
as they prepared for confrontation. When energy was exhausted in

frantic planning, they did not attend to other interests and relationships, so their lives narrowed progressively. Now you plan your life instead of just reacting to problems. Patience allows you to work steadily and see plans and dreams become reality. Balanced planning yields a feeling of purpose and direction. You make life happen instead of waiting to respond to the next crisis. Others can count on you to plan and follow through.

Freedom from Frantic Thinking

Agitation became so pervasive that the money addicts never could relax. Their minds jumped from one thought to another; they could make no sense of their experience, nor could they plan their future. Recovery allows you to focus as you make decisions and stay honest one day at a time. Freedom from frantic thinking allows your problem solving abilities to flourish and grow. Clarity means control of thinking, judgment, and reasoning powers.

Freedom from Intellectual and Creative Stagnation

The money addicts didn't have the time and attention to learn new things or nurture their imagination, so they stopped growing while they cultivated their addiction. During recovery you become better acquainted with your special gifts and talents and new ways to express what you are. You rediscover old interests and develop new ones. You find hidden talents and ambitions.

Freedom from Dishonest Relationships

The money addicts' lives, including their relationships, were founded in deception. Release from past obsession makes you available to yourself and others and opens you to the challenge of honesty in human relationships. As you face yourself and your compulsive spending, you can make amends to the people you have hurt by your addiction. Relationships heal in the new climate. If some relationships never heal, you can at least take comfort in knowing that you honestly tried.

Freedom from Overcontrol

The money addicts drain themselves in the fruitless effort to restrain compulsions that have escaped their control. They divert themselves from their own powerlessness by seeking to govern everyone and everything else. In recovery, you let go of this struggle and become more comfortable with not always having all of the answers. You learn to accept ambiguity and uncertainty in your life. The more you trust yourself and others, the more you can focus on living your own life well.

Freedom from Emotional Death

The money addicts' emotions were extreme cycles of fear, guilt, and depression, with sudden shifts from one mood to another. They dampened the pain with numbness. Living in the emotional whirlwind of compulsive spending numbed and paralyzed their complete range of feelings. All of your feelings, including calm, return as you work toward honesty about money and its place in your life. Feelings can work for you or against you. Dealing with your money problems also means dealing with the pain associated with these problems. Through counseling and Twelve Step programs you begin to uncover and heal your feelings. The more you know about yourself, the more free your emotional life becomes. Learning to embrace and make friends with your feelings is one gift of recovery. You can have freedom and joy instead of pain and compulsion.

Freedom from Spiritual Deprivation

The misery of addiction robbed people of the grace and peaceful freedom possible only in a spiritual life. Spiritual freedom embraces all of the other seven freedoms and wraps them in a blanket of serenity. In recovery, you come to believe that there is a power greater than yourself. For some of you, that power is God, for some it's the power of nature or the power of the fellowship of DA; a room full of recovering people is more powerful than just one. Recovery renews your spiritual self, whether or not formal religion is part of your life. Although your world cannot ever be without trouble, your spirit can be safe, whatever adversity comes. Spiritual freedom is the final gift of recovery that brings you back to yourself and others.

CHAPTER

17

Money Success for Children

The old value of setting financial goals has lost much of its meaning in today's era of consumerism. Problems in money management and compulsive spending have reached epidemic proportions in our society as children are taught to become adults who buy now and pay later. Kids see their parents receive cash from machines. They are bombarded with television commercials that show other children on expensive vacations and playing with expensive toys. Many four year olds are aware of brand names, clothing labels, and status automobiles. They tell Mom, "It said on TV to buy it today!" or "Please it's part of a nutritious breakfast! They said so on TV." When a child is told "We can't afford it," he often responds, "Then go to the money machine!"

One father said his child told a neighbor friend, "Put the ball on my deck." The father explained to the five year old that they didn't have a deck on their house, it was actually a stoop. The girl was devastated. "What do you mean we don't have a deck? Everyone has a deck. How come we have a stoop!" Trying to soften the blow, the father said, "A stoop is just as good. Besides, we can't afford to build a deck." The child considered this statement. "Well, borrow the money then," she said. She had learned by the age of five that if you can't afford something, you should borrow against tomorrow.

Children's toys no longer are sold primarily at small, neighborhood shops but in jumbo, two-story warehouses where a small, inexpensive doll pales beside the seemingly endless array of motorized, computerized, high-tech children's playthings. The days are gone when a two-wheeler was the high point of childhood. Now children want more and better things, just like their parents. It's harder than ever to put *things* in some sort of healthy perspective. Parents today are challenged to teach their children how to use money wisely. They can learn skills that lay the foundation of successful money management. The following suggestions will help.

Share Money Secrets

Sharing financial information regarding the family budget, financial goals, and priorities sets the stage for a healthy understanding and appreciation for the use of money. As they mature, children can understand the concepts of income, expenses, and savings. When children understand that the family budget isn't primarily for recreation, they accept family financial limitations as a necessary reality. Parents who explain the family's financial responsibilities without blame or guilt set a powerful example about money, honesty, and trust. Children feel a sense of power and pride in being a part of this vital aspect of family living.

Teach Successful Saving and Spending

Lessons about saving and spending necessarily begin at an early age. Children can learn that making money decisions brings consequences. The use of "now and later jars" is one technique. The child labels two clear containers "Now" and "Later" and chooses to deposit money in either jar. Now money can be spent at any time, but Later money accumulates until a goal is reached, such as three dollars for a toy. The money goal should be realistic and written on a piece of paper and deposited in the Later jar. This simple method teaches a hands-on lesson about choices everyone makes about money as well as the experience of financial goal-setting and the discipline of delayed gratification. The discipline provides a natural bridge to opening a savings account. Parents praise realistic goal-setting and discourage money games such as borrowing from the Later jar to meet immediate needs.

Expose "Money Magic" Myths

Credit and bank cards, checking accounts, and other forms of money exchange make it difficult for children to understand how saving and spending really work. Money magically appears at the cash machine. To dispel misconceptions, parents might walk their children through a tour of the financial world. Starting with a parent's paycheck, they trace its path to the bank, pointing out the vault where the money is kept. Using a pretend check and play money, the child and parent play store, removing money from the account and depositing it in the store's account after it goes to the bank. This game allows the child to see the pile of play money diminish when checks are written against the paycheck, cash is withdrawn from money machines, and credit card bills are paid. Information about savings and compounding interest also can be taught. When the child is sufficiently mature, the parent can help her open a savings account.

Teach Honesty

In order to make healthy money decisions, children need to learn honesty in their use of money. Flash card stories can help. On each of five flash cards write a story about money; on the back, write several possible solutions to a problem the story poses. The front of a flash card might say "Louise wants to buy a new dress for her Barbie doll, but her mother says she can't fit it into her budget this month." The back of the card lists possible solutions:

1. Forget about buying the dress for now.
2. Ask Dad for the money when Mom isn't around.
3. Save allowance for the dress.
4. Do extra chores or work to earn the money.
5. Borrow the money.
6. Other.

With more than two choices, a child can think in terms of options rather than all or nothing extremes. The parent can help her talk over the consequences of each possible decision, thereby encouraging creative thought about money matters.

The puzzles increase in difficulty as the child matures and becomes accustomed to this reasoning process. Children should not be scolded or lectured for selecting poor choices. Instead encourage them to continue to play this game and reason out consequences.

Avoid Making Money an Emotional Weapon

Money becomes a problem when it is seen as a measure of success or failure, strength or weakness, goodness or badness, and reward or punishment. Associated with these qualities, money may take on emotional power in childhood. The list could go on forever: "You've been such a good girl. Santa will bring you a lot of presents." Or "You didn't do the dishes, so I'm not going to give you money to go to the movies with your friends." Or "It costs so much money to raise you—why aren't you more grateful?" The message the child receives is clear: If you're good, you get rewarded with material things; if you neglect your duties, you are deprived of money.

Linked with reward and punishment, money becomes a powerful emotional factor. When it is presented primarily as a useful form of exchange for services and goods, money becomes a helpful ally instead of an emotional dragon.

Agree on Allowance and Money Goals

Children receive from parents a united view of finances in family life. A pattern of parental money fights, manipulations, and disagreements teaches children that money is emotional rather than utilitarian in its primary purpose. Parents are challenged to resolve their own money issues and then work together on a program of financial awareness for their children. A united front is essential to set up allowances. Most experts agree that it is not helpful to link allowances with household chores.

Children seem to respond better to chores when they learn that chores are a privilege and a necessary responsibility of each family member. The reward is in the accomplishment of the task as well as the feeling of generosity and doing one's part. Parents may need to work hard at not punishing with money deprivation.

Model Delays in Gratification

When money regularly is used to fill emotional needs and voids, it becomes a "quick fix" for ailments. Modern American culture promotes instant gratification and comfort at any cost. Children who learn to comfort themselves with a purchase conclude that relief for their feelings can be bought. Children are happier when they are experienced in tackling difficulty. A patient attitude is an excellent model for children. When parents wait in a grocery line without complaining, they teach children to tolerate discomfort without having to fix it instantly. Parents who seem content with their lives while they wait and plan to buy a new car or other needed item teach children to respect the necessity of time in the accomplishment of goals. If parents model delayed spending, children develop the same capacity.

Teach Children to Make Friends with Boredom

Life is dull sometimes. Sadly, our culture tends to view quiet times as boring and depressing. Many people engage in frantic activity to avoid solitude. They use food, sex, alcohol, cigarettes, and money to ward off boredom. Parents who teach children to relax and engage in quiet activities and enjoy their own company enable them to enjoy the normal ebb and flow. Money as an emotional escape becomes less attractive to children who regularly feel fulfilled.

Avoid Monopoly Thinking

Money is not a game that can change at any moment with the luck of the dice. Get-rich-quick and rags-to-riches myths take money as a product of luck instead of work and planning. Monopoly thinking teaches that no matter how big the problem, money can buy the way "out of jail." Appealing as these attitudes are, they are harmful to children.

Teach Thoughtful Spending

Parents who are impulsive spenders teach their children to have the same unstructured habits with money. Help children take time to think through money decisions. Thoughtful spending is shopping and spending at a relaxed, comfortable pace, with careful consideration of purchases. Initially parents may have difficulty slowing down grocery and shopping trips, but the results will be bountiful for them and their children if they do so.

Teach the Pitfalls of Spending for Status

Nothing is wrong with children's desire to wear the same kinds of jeans as the other kids in the class. The danger comes when children view money and material goods as primary indicators of popularity, personal goodness, and measures of value. Wise parents help their children explore and fill deeper inner needs while recognizing needs for peer acceptance. A child who feels inadequate will never be healed solely by identifying with peers. Families who talk, share, and validate find that their happiness and feelings of worth don't depend on material possessions.

Teach Repayment of Debts

Most people in our society have borrowed money in their lives. Children can learn integrity by borrowing money and paying it back on time. Parents who want to teach this principle must honor their own debts responsibly. If you borrow a small amount of money from your child, give her a written IOU with the written date of repayment.

Promptly pay back the loan on the promised date and collect the IOU. You might then sit with your child and play a game. "Imagine how you might have felt if I hadn't paid you back when I said I would. Also, imagine how I might have felt if I hadn't kept my promise." Such experiences teach a child practical information about the responsible use of money.

Be Generous with Your Time and Measured with Money

Children need to feel that their parents have time for them and that they enjoy their company. Parents who practice being generous and positive with their time and attention enable their children to feel valued for who they are instead of for what material possessions they have. The richest gift a parent can give a child is a personal, affirming relationship. Parents who feel they were deprived in their own childhoods may need to heal their losses before they can give generously of themselves to their own children.

Teach the Value of Vocational Satisfaction

The value of satisfying work transcends the value of money. Parents can model their joy with their own attitudes. A father who hums while he does the dishes teaches a different message than one who slams and bangs pots and pans. Obviously parents who feel challenged and gratified by their work can pass along this positive message more readily than people whose work frustrates them. Sometimes parents direct children toward high-paying occupations and forget the need of each child to find his or her own path. It is satisfying to find an enjoyable vocation that is also financially lucrative, though such a fit may not happen for everybody. Parents who teach the privilege and joy of work that is emotionally rewarding help their children make good decisions about their futures.

Validate and Praise Decisions about Money

Children benefit from praise for their ability to make decisions about money. A vital part of learning and growing is their certain and unavoidable mistakes. Parents who praise their children regularly make it easier for them to accept constructive criticism. Those who are repeatedly shamed and criticized feel devalued and powerless. Often they turn their energy into anger and self-destructive behavior.

Parents who are in a pattern of regular criticism may need professional counseling to learn how to be more positive with their children. Children need an affirming and positive relationship with a parent in order to feel secure enough to evaluate bad money decisions and change their behavior accordingly.

Model Prosperity Thinking

Prosperity thinkers expect to meet adequately all of their financial needs. This attitude stresses the concept of abundance. Thoughts are self-fulfilling prophecies that define the world; to some degree we bring them into reality. Parents can learn to change their pessimism to affirmation. Here are examples of cynicism or a dismal view of life, stances that hurt children:

- I'll never make enough money to get out of debt.
- I'm not a very good or talented person because I don't make a lot of money.
- My children drain all of my energy and money.
- Money makes the world go around.
- You can never be too rich or too thin.
- I can't play with you now; I've got to work to make money to support you.

Some contrasting affirmations are:

- My debt is not permanent.
- I make money easily.
- My children fill me with pride. The rewards of parenting exceed the costs.

- Money can't buy happiness, but happiness can bring more money.
- I am perfectly all right, exactly as I am today.
- You are not a burden.

Prosperity thinking replaces thoughts of lack and scarcity with the hope-filled expectations of fulfillment and abundance. When parents start to believe that they will have the resources to survive, they begin to see positive solutions to problems that used to baffle them. As they step away from negative thinking, they put their money and other life problems into perspective. Consciously changing their thought patterns by focusing on the positive creates a feeling of gratitude and hope. Parents teach their children through their attitudes and reactions. As they learn to be positive thinkers, they become free to make decisions about their finances. Positive attitudes will be their children's best lesson about money.

18

How to Help Someone Who Has a Money Addiction

It hurts to see someone you care for poison life with money addiction. If she cared, you think, she would stop. She must want to live like this, or else she would stop. Chances are you've already tried nagging, hinting, scolding, threatening, and attacking and found that none of it worked. Some things, however, do help. At least you can learn to react in ways that don't aggravate the problem.

Helpful Things to Do

Do speak in "I" statements. Tell your friend or relative how the behavior affects you and makes you feel. Don't say "You're so selfish; look at everything you bought!" Instead say "I get scared when I see how much you buy, because we don't have the money to pay for it." In expressing how you feel (scared about the behavior) and why (because you don't have the money), you keep the focus on you, your feelings, and your observations rather than the other person. If the one you love feels judged or attacked, she cannot hear what you most want to say. On the other hand, if she perceives your sharing something about yourself, you stand a better chance of being understood.

Do allow others to feel the natural consequences of their behavior. If Mary keeps giving money to Dick whenever he can't meet his expenses, she deprives him of the opportunity to experience the result of his behavior. If, on the other hand, she says no to his request, she gives him the chance to see the reality of his behavior. Only when someone feels some consequences does he wish to change.

Do stay true to your own standards and values. If you believe cheating is wrong, don't be an accomplice to someone's illegal scheme to get money. If you don't generally lie, don't start now by making excuses for your loved one's actions.

Do set limits. Make your own intentions clear. Tell the money addict, "If you get evicted from your apartment, I will not put you up," or "I'm not going to allow you to take my vacation away. If you want to spend your half of the cost on other things, that's your decision, but I'm taking the vacation as planned."

Do continue leading a full life. The best thing you can do to help another is not to allow her to draw you into her illness. Continue enjoying your normal activities, getting enough rest and exercise, and eating well. If you become wrapped up in the problem, you become part of the problem.

Harmful Things to Avoid

If you do the helpful things described above, you will not fall into the trap of insulating a money addict from the consequences of his behavior, thereby helping him to stay sick. Avoid the following enabling behaviors:

Don't minimize. A person who downplays the consequences of a compulsive spender's behavior denies the reality of her own feelings and circumstances. "Things aren't really so bad" and "Lots of other people have problems worse than ours" are minimizing statements.

Don't justify. Some people continually search for ways to make sense of the painful reality in their lives: "My sister is used to nice things; she was raised that way." Justification is an attempt to validate behavior or actions by finding an acceptable reason for unacceptable behavior.

Don't protect. Money addicts' friends and relatives often lose their sense of separation and individuality and end up suffering when the spenders suffer. They become enmeshed in addicts' lives, losing themselves in the process. Protectors shield the compulsive spenders from the logical negative consequences of their actions. These enablers often go to extraordinary lengths to protect and hide the true reality of a negative situation. Denial eases extreme pain and defends the spouse or the friend from knowledge of the threatening truth. Some people have a stake in maintaining the money addicts' compulsion, lest their own behavior come under scrutiny.

Don't control. Relatives may take charge and "fix" spenders' problems by masterminding elaborate plans and schemes to save them from negative consequences. These controlling persons always seem to be prominent in whatever problem occurs in the lives of compulsive spenders. They believe that everything would be okay if they were in charge. Often very emotional and demanding, controllers are energized and excited by the drama in the world of a compulsive spender. They have to learn to live their own lives.

Don't spend with the overspender. Money addicts may involve others in their compulsive behavior in order to legitimize it. Sometimes a friend or spouse spends with the spender in anger or despair. People who regularly join in a money addiction should take an honest look at their own behavior to see whether they, too, have a problem.

Don't blame and lecture. Lectures give the compulsive spender a reason to stay angry at the lecturer. The time and energy devoted to anger and irritation distracts their attention from their real problems and helps them to ignore what is being said.

Don't deny. The belief that the compulsive spender's problem isn't real allows a significant other to put his head in the sand. It ignores the seriousness of the spender's problem and the effects it has on others' lives. Denial is the umbrella that arches over all of the other enabling behaviors.

Don't endure and wait. Some people feel that putting up with negative behavior is the best solution. They martyr themselves, hoping that time will cure all wounds and fix all problems. Self-pity becomes a depressing cloak that may complicate the loved one's recovery from compulsive spending.

Enabling behaviors develop as survival techniques that make a painful situation more livable or bearable. Unaddressed problems worsen, however, in the resulting atmosphere of denied and unexpressed feelings. An enabler is drawn by stages into the web of the money addiction. Initially the enabler denies the reality of the situation and may enjoy the experience of shopping with and receiving gifts from the buyer. A growing ability to rationalize helps the enabler to deny the mounting stack of bills and the money worries it brings. She eventually loses respect for herself as well as the addict. She feels inadequate and hopeless about her inability to change the buyer, who may shame and abuse her. She begins to wonder whether, in fact, she isn't to blame for everything. Ultimately enmeshed in the addiction, the enabler loses self-esteem and objectivity.

Self-exploration and education about addiction releases an enabler from imprisonment in a loved one's addiction. Her recovery necessitates the realization that the power to improve her own life lies in reacting more honestly to the spender.

What You "Give Up" to Stop Enabling

As you begin to understand that you are powerful and can change enabling reactions into healthy responses, identify and mourn the loss of ways in which you "liked" and used enabling:

Superior Feelings
Being the "good guy" in a relationship is emotionally seductive. You may have to focus more on your own life if you give up your obsession with the buyer. Sometimes this shift of attention is very scary.

Hidden Financial Irresponsibility
When someone else's spending is out of control, you can easily hide your own.

False Feelings of Power and Control
Manipulation, worry, and efforts to manage may give you a false sense of power in your life. If you stopped enabling, what would you do with your time and energy?

The Roller Coaster Drama
As much as you sometimes may hate the continual crisis, people who

"live on the edge" with money addicts get hooked on the ups and downs of escape and rescue.

A Head-in-the-Sand Attitude about the Relationship
When you stop enabling, you have plenty of time and energy to consider the reality of your relationship. Is it intimate? Does it meet both of your needs? Many enablers go to great lengths consciously and subconsciously to avoid asking such difficult questions.

Formal Interventions

In intervention, a money addict's friends and family confront him about his pattern of destructive behavior, specifically describing the injurious effects on them, stating personal standards and bottom lines and recommending ways to get help. A formal intervention is a planned and rehearsed event carried out with a professional counselor's help. Significant persons in the money addict's life explain how the compulsions have hurt them. The purpose of an intervention is to break through the wall of denial and to present a treatment plan.

Interventions have been used successfully in the addiction field for many years. The preparation and attitudes of the team usually determine the likely outcome. This fact makes competent, professional guidance essential. Many counselors feel that a carefully prepared intervention is always a success, regardless of whether the addict accepts treatment; the process helps the family and friends to be honest about the situation, to begin their own recovery, and to mourn the losses that always attend life with a money addict. Success is assured when intervention members focus on the process of the experience instead of the outcome.

Acknowledge the Problem
Be honest about the spender's out-of-control behavior and its effects. Families and friends sometimes become numb to the buyer's loss of control. Simply listing the damages helps focus the problem and exposes the pattern.

Get Professional Help

Interventions are more successful when an objective and informed intervention counselor is present. Find one who has experience with interventions. Your counselor will help you decide whether you are ready to plan an intervention or whether you need to prepare yourself with personal counseling. When both you and your counselor are ready, your counselor will help you select appropriate people to join the intervention team.

Form an Intervention Team

An intervention team usually comprises two to eight members, people close to the money addict who are aware of the pain caused by her behavior. They may include family, friends, employers, clergy, creditors, or others.

Encourage Participants to be Trusting and Willing

Attending the first meeting to plan the intervention takes a lot of courage. Team members may feel unsure why they're there. They may be embarrassed or afraid that the intervention will not work. These natural feelings need to be expressed openly in the preparatory meetings. Participants must be trusting and willing enough to face a tense encounter in pain and uncertainty but caring enough to participate nevertheless.

Tell the Whole Story

Everyone on the team needs an opportunity to tell about all of their experiences with the compulsive buyer. Years of bottled up feelings often spill forth in the initial planning meetings. The counselor validates the team members' feelings and experiences, letting them know that the intervention is as much for them as it is for the person they care about.

Work with the Grief

Participants who have lived in the web of compulsive buying often feel confused and ashamed. They also may experience a deep sense of inadequacy and failure: "If only I had. . . ."

This shame and guilt cripples caring people and saps their personal energy and power. As the counselor encourages the team to talk about their mutual feelings, they begin to heal some of the wounds inflicted by shame. The intervention team comes to understand the powerful dynamics of compulsive buying, learning how their "good intentions" and "forced solutions" produced few positive results and usually enabled the compulsive buyer to rationalize continued buying. The honest sharing of feelings and the new establishment of personal boundaries will bring energy and hope to the team.

Team members can learn to become responsible *to* others instead of responsible *for* them. The three Cs of addiction start to make sense: "They didn't cause it, they can't cure it, and they can't control it." The people around the money addict learn that they have the power and resources to change their own lives and reactions to the compulsive buyer.

Gain Hope through Education

After telling their stories and after beginning to mourn the past, team members learn about the process of addiction and how it relates to compulsive buying. They learn about phases, signs, symptoms, and progression of the problem as well as myths about addiction and the hope of recovery.

Plan the Intervention and the
Continuing Action of the Team Members

The counselor helps the team prepare the intervention, at the same time developing a plan of action for themselves and the compulsive buyer. The compulsive buyer comes to the intervention session by invitation. Each participant reads a script that specifies the compulsive spender's activities and behavior and shows how they have directly affected the team member. Each experience begins with "I" statements and avoids blaming or attacking. For example: "I was embarrassed when my friends saw our car being repossessed."

One by one the team members read their statements. Their hope is that the compulsive buyer may understand the reality of his behavior and how it affects his life and the lives of others. The counselor asks team members to recommend a treatment and recovery plan to the compulsive buyer, to state specifically how their own enabling behaviors will change, and to establish new boundaries with the compulsive buyer. One might say for example, "I will no longer lie to creditors when they call and ask about you."

Surrender to the Outcome

As they approach the intervention, the counselor may remind the team that trust and surrender are crucial, since the outcome is not in their hands. Freedom, direction, and personal power will be present in the intervention session of a well-rehearsed team. It is important to attend a follow-up session so that everyone has an opportunity to talk about the effects of the intervention experience.

Take Care of Yourself

The primary purpose of the intervention is to provide an opportunity for the team to learn new and loving ways to take care of themselves. These plans need a firm commitment so the members can begin to live in serenity. Peace of mind depends on ongoing determination to reject unacceptable behavior from the compulsive spender in their lives.

Informal Intervention

Even without the intercession of a counselor, one or more persons may sit down with the money addict and speak from the heart about the effect of his behavior. The meeting is not an attack session. An addict's friends and family must clearly care if the intervention is to do any good. The informal intervention team needs to rehearse the meeting and practice their expression of caring and the specific details of their experience with the addict. They should approach the money addict with some suggestions such as attendance at DA meetings or meeting with a counselor who knows about money addiction.

CHAPTER

19

Ginny's Story—Conclusion

As Ginny's spending became more ungovernable, her beliefs and values disintegrated as well. A few years earlier, she had considered lying, cheating, and stealing to be despicable behaviors. In the face of mounting debt and continuous panic, Ginny's standards collapsed.

One evening her husband, Noel, came home from work with disturbing news. An employee of his construction company had stolen a blank signed check and cashed it for $200. Since it was written to cash and endorsed with a company stamp, Noel had no doubt who did it. His secretary, Gloria, was the only one who had a key to the safe in which the checks were kept and who had access to the endorsement stamp. What particularly disturbed Noel was the fact that Gloria had worked for him faithfully for sixteen years. He trusted her and was fond of her.

What Noel didn't consider was the fact that Ginny also had access to everything. Noel kept spare office keys at home in the desk. Ginny was torn. If she confessed, the shame might be unbearable. A horrible scene could be the end of everything. Noel might become violent or go on a drinking binge and hurt himself or someone else. He probably would divorce her; if he didn't, he would never again believe a word she said. On the other hand, if she kept quiet, an innocent, dedicated worker would be unjustly accused and fired.

Ginny decided to try to shift the blame. "Couldn't a stranger have broken in and taken the check?"

"No," said Noel. "Nothing had been disturbed, it was someone with a key."

At that point Ginny considered suicide. She was absolutely sure that she couldn't face this dilemma. She felt defeated, hopeless, and completely worthless. But when she thought of her children, she realized that she couldn't leave them motherless. Somehow, for them, she had to survive. She asked Noel to delay action for a few days, until every last possibility was ruled out. To her surprise, he agreed.

A few days later, Noel came home in the middle of a workday. He was eerily rigid and controlled. At first she thought he was drunk but quickly realized that he was stone cold sober. He asked Ginny to call Cathy, the neighbor, immediately and ask her to watch the children for a while. When Noel would not tell Ginny where he was taking her, she was frightened and confused. She pleaded for an explanation, but Noel was silent. He just drove her to an unknown destination, which turned out to be the bank.

"Why are we here?" Ginny whispered as she followed Noel through the bank, past all of the tellers and the loan officers to the office of the bank president, who was also Noel's golf partner on Wednesdays. For an instant she felt a glimmer of hope that maybe, somehow, this mystery was all a wonderful surprise Noel was going to spring on her. When he opened the heavy wooden door without even knocking, the illusion evaporated.

Seated around a large conference table were a varied group of people the bank president, Gloria from Noel's office, a bank teller named Annalee, and a gray-haired lady Ginny didn't think she knew. Noel did. He said, "Ginny, you know everyone here, please sit down and watch the TV."

Ginny saw that everyone's eyes were cast down, as if they were all embarrassed for her. She lowered herself into the chair and located the TV on the mahogany chest. The others' chairs were all arranged to afford an uninterrupted view of the TV.

Noel turned on the TV. It was a videotape of the bank. People were standing in lines before the tellers, customers were sitting alongside the desks of bank officers in conference, and suddenly Ginny wanted to throw up. There she was, being waited on by Annalee. She was wearing that turquoise skirt and sweater and dark glasses, cashing the check.

Epilogue

Ginny's story has no ending. Nor do our own life stories. If we're lucky, we get today. What we choose to do with these twenty-four hours is our decision. The worst we can do is choose unhappiness and self-destruction. The best? Well, the best we can do has no limits or definitions. Ginny is wounded. She needs to heal. She needs to mend from the inside out. Most of us want to mend from the outside in. We try, but we end up with more of the same more wounds, more misery. We need to begin the healing from within, from our hearts and minds and spirits, knowing that, while we cannot fix others, we do have the power to fix ourselves. With this knowledge, we are on our way toward personal freedom.

Ginny has learned to feel inadequate, unaccepted, incapable, and unlovable. She creates situations that substantiate her feelings. She can unlearn that self-image. She can have a life rich in confidence, love, and inner peace. She also can decide to have an abundance of wealth, both spiritual and material, without the shame. She can be happy in the stillness of her life as well as the busy times.

She can detach from Noel's alcoholism problem and concentrate on her own problem. Whether he, too, chooses recovery is his decision alone. Regardless of Noel's or anyone else's behavior, she can be spiritually intact, whole, and healthy. The child within her that never knew unconditional love and acceptance can take comfort now in the knowledge that someone dependable and accepting is in charge now. Her name is Ginny!

About the Authors

Sally Coleman, who has more than twenty years of counseling experience, is staff psychotherapist and coordinator of addictions services at the University of Notre Dame's Counseling Center, where she provides individual and group psychotherapy. She is an adult-children group facilitator and trainer; trains interns and doctoral students in addictions; presents workshops and trains professionals to help people cope with grief; and facilitates therapy groups for clergy.

A graduate of Marquette University, Milwaukee, with a master's degree in counseling psychology from the University of Notre Dame, she is certified nationally as an addictions counselor. She is a former Michigan coordinator of Parkside Lutheran Center for Substance Abuse in Park Ridge, Illinois.

Sally Coleman is the coauthor of several books, *Seasons of the Spirit*, meditations for midlife and beyond, *Our Best Days*, and *Lifework: A Workbook for Adult Children of Alcoholics*.

Nancy Hull-Mast is a freelance writer with training in addictions counseling. She worked for two years as a counselor in an inpatient setting. Later she was employed as an addictions prevention specialist, working with youth and parents.

Now she devotes herself to writing about social issues. She created screenplays for twelve films about addiction that won numerous awards for creative excellence. One film has been translated into several foreign languages and is distributed internationally. Another is among the best-selling films that have been produced on this subject. She is the recipient of many writing awards, including the CINE

Golden Eagle and the National Council on Family Relations Film Festival Award.

Nancy Hull-Mast is the author of eight educational pamphlets on addiction and coauthor of two books, *Our Best Days*, book of meditations for youth, and *Sibs*, for siblings of young addicts.

Appendix

Spending Choices Plan Worksheet

Monthly Salary: _____

Column 1	Column 2	Column 3	Column 4
Items	Current Expenses	New Choices	Actual Expenses (After Implementing Plan)
Rent or mortgage	_____	_____	_____
Utilities	_____	_____	_____
Food	_____	_____	_____
Transportation	_____	_____	_____
Clothing	_____	_____	_____
Medical	_____	_____	_____
Household	_____	_____	_____
Laundry	_____	_____	_____
Cleaning	_____	_____	_____
Taxes	_____	_____	_____
Personal	_____	_____	_____
Entertainment	_____	_____	_____
Business expenses	_____	_____	_____
Recreation	_____	_____	_____
Education	_____	_____	_____
Insurance	_____	_____	_____
Bank credit cards	_____	_____	_____
	_____	_____	_____
	_____	_____	_____
	_____	_____	_____
	_____	_____	_____

Column 1	Column 2	Column 3	Column 4
Items	Current Expenses	New Choices	Actual Expenses (After Implementing Plan)
Department store credit cards			
Gas credit cards			
Personal loans			
Other loans			
Misc. (such as pets, news-papers)			

Column 1	Column 2	Column 3	Column 4
Items	Current Expenses	New Choices	Actual Expenses (After Implementing Plan)
Other			
	_____	_____	_____
	_____	_____	_____
	_____	_____	_____
	_____	_____	_____
	_____	_____	_____
	_____	_____	_____
	_____	_____	_____
	_____	_____	_____
	_____	_____	_____
	_____	_____	_____

Ways to Add Income

Idea	Amount ($)
1.	
2.	
3.	
4.	
5.	
6.	
7.	
8.	
9.	
10.	
11.	
12.	
13.	
14.	
15.	
16.	
17.	
18.	
19.	
20.	

Ways to Reduce Expenses

Idea	Amount ($)
1. _____	_____
2. _____	_____
3. _____	_____
4. _____	_____
5. _____	_____
6. _____	_____
7. _____	_____
8. _____	_____
9. _____	_____
10. _____	_____
11. _____	_____
12. _____	_____
13. _____	_____
14. _____	_____
15. _____	_____
16. _____	_____
17. _____	_____
18. _____	_____
19. _____	_____
20. _____	_____

Summary Worksheet

1. Total monthly salary $_____
    Minus total column 2   (-)_____
    This figure can be negative or positive   (=)_____

    _____

2. Total amount from "Ways to Add Income" $_____
    Plus total income   (+)_____

    _____

3. Total of no. 2 $_____
    Plus total from "Ways to Reduce Expenses" (+)_____
                                                     (=)_____

4. If your final total still does not agree with your monthly income,
    you can keep working with your ideas for adding income and
    reducing expenses to bring it closer. Debtors Anonymous and
    credit counseling services are invaluable help in devising a liv-
    able plan for spending your money.

The Twelve Steps of Alcoholics Anonymous

1. We admitted we were powerless over alcohol—that our lives had become unmanageable.
2. Came to believe that a Power greater than ourselves could restore us to sanity.
3. Made a decision to turn our will and our lives over to the care of God, as we understood him.
4. Made a searching and fearless moral inventory of ourselves.
5. Admitted to God, to ourselves, and to another human being the exact nature of our wrongs.
6. Were entirely ready to have God remove all these defects of character.
7. Humbly asked Him to remove our shortcomings.
8. Made a list of all persons we had harmed, and became willing to make amends to them all.
9. Made direct amends to such people wherever possible, except when to do so would injure them or others.
10. Continued to take personal inventory and when we were wrong, promptly admitted it.
11. Sought through prayer and meditation to improve our conscious contact with God, as we understood Him, praying only for knowledge of His will for us and the power to carry that out.
12. Having had a spiritual awakening as the result of these Steps, we tried to carry this message to alcoholics, and to practice these principles in all our affairs.

The Twelve Steps are reprinted with permission of Alcoholics Anonymous World Services, Inc. Permission to reprint does not mean that AA has reviewed or approved the content of this publication, nor that AA agrees with the views expressed herein. AA is a program of recovery from alcoholism—use of the Twelve Steps in connection with programs and activities that are patterned after AA, but that address other problems does not imply otherwise.

Resources

Suggested Readings

Blue, R., and J. Blue. 1988. *Money matters for parents and their kids*. Nashville: Oliver-Nelson.

Bradshaw, J. 1988. *Healing the shame that binds you* Deerfield Beach, Fla.: Health Communications.

Coleman, S. 1982. Dollars and Sense in Recovery. *Alcoholism Magazine*, Jan.-Feb., 55.

Coleman, S., and R. J. Donley. 1992. *Lifework*. Minneapolis: CompCare.

Damon, J. E. 1988. *Shopaholics*. Los Angeles: Price Stern Sloan.

Gawain, S. 1978. Meditations: *Creative visualization and meditation exercises to enrich your life*. San Rafael, Calif.: New World Library

Givens, C. 1991. *More wealth without risk*. New York: Simon and Schuster.

Hay, L. L. 1984. *You can heal your life*. Santa Monica, Calif.: Hay House.

Jampolsky, G. G. 1979. *Love is letting go of fear*. New York: Bantam Books.

Jellinek, E. M. 1960. *The disease concept of alcoholism*. New Haven, Conn.: Yale University Press.

Johnson, V. E. 1973. *I'll quit tomorrow*. New York: Harper and Row.

_____. 1986. *Intervention: How to help someone who doesn't want help*. Minneapolis: Johnson Institute.

Kehrer, D. 1988. How to Get Out of Debt. *Changing Times*, April.

Larsen, E. 1987. *Stage II relationships: Love beyond addiction*. San Francisco: Harper and Row.

Lerner H. G. 1989. *The dance of intimacy*. New York: HarperCollins.

McAleese, T. 1991. *Money: How to get it, keep it, and make it grow*. Hawthorne, N.J.: Career Press.

Morris, B. 1987. Big Spenders: As a Favored Pastime, Shopping Ranks High with Most Americans. *Wall Street Journal*, July 30.

Mundis, J. 1988. *How to get out of debt, stay out of debt, and live prosperously*. New York: Bantam.

Nibley, M. 1989. Compulsive Spenders Face Addictions. *South Bend Tribune*, Oct. 6.

Norwood, R. 1985. *Women who love too much*. New York: St. Martin's.

Peterson, K. S. 1990. Disputes Can Put Mates on Shaky Ground: Creative Ways to Avoid Checkbook Fights. *USA Today*, April

Ponder, C. 1962. *The dynamic laws of prosperity*. Englewood Cliffs, N.J.: Prentice-Hall.

Potter-Efron, R., and P. Potter-Efron. 1989. *I deserve respect: Finding and healing shame in personal relationships*. Center City, Minn.: Hazelden.

Power, J. 1969. *Why am I afraid to tell you who I am?* Allen, Tex.: Argus.

Randle, W. 1989. When the Going Gets Tough, It's Time to Stop Shopping. *Chicago Tribune*, Nov. 2.

Reiners, K. 1980. *There's more to life than pumpkins, drugs and other false gods.* Wayzata, Minn.: Woodland.

Rosellini, G., and M. Worden. 1985. *Of course you're angry.* Center City, Minn.: Hazelden.

Rubenstein, C. 1989. Smart Money: Ignorance Is No Longer Bliss. Women Are Seeking Financial Expertise and Economic Independence. *Ms.*, Nov.

Viorst, J. 1986. *Necessary losses.* New York: Simon and Schuster.

Wegscheider-Cruse, S. 1987. *Learning to love yourself* Pompano Beach, Fla.: Health Communications.

Woititz, J. G. 1985. *Struggle for intimacy.* Pompano Beach, Fla.: Health Communications.

Notes

1. Sally Coleman, "Dollars and Sense in Recovery," *Alcoholism Magazine*, Jan.-Feb. 1982, 55.

2. Mary Wisniewski, "Bankruptcies Here Rise but Fail to Match Increases in Northeast," *Daily Law Bulletin* 138, Chicago, IU. (Jan. 21, 1992): 2.

3. Anne Wilson Schaef, *When Society Becomes an Addict* (San Francisco: Harper, 1988), 22.

4. Gerald G. May, M.D., *Addiction and Grace* (San Francisco: Harper, 1988), 50.

5. Patrick Carnes, *Out of the Shadows* (Minneapolis: CompCare, 1983), ii.

6. Daniel M. Kehrer, "How to Cut Out Debt," *Changing Times*, April, 1988, 23-27.

7. Sally Coleman and Rita J. Donley, *Lifework* (Notre Dame, Ind.: Ave Maria Press, 1990), 5.